LETTING
GOD
HELP
YOU

JOHN A. REDHEAD

LETTING

GOD

HELP

YOU

ABINGDON PRESS

NASHVILLE • NEW YORK

LETTING GOD HELP YOU

ISBN 0-687-21618-4

Library of Congress Catalog Card Number: 57-11014

SET UP, PRINTED, AND BOUND BY THE
PARTHENON PRESS, AT NASHVILLE,
TENNESSEE, UNITED STATES OF AMERICA

TO MY WIFE

A Pleasant Companion on
the Pathway to Power

PREFACE

Dr. H. H. Farmer of Cambridge writes that when God comes to a person he comes in two ways. The first is "unconditional demand," and the second is "final succor." The dictionary defines "succor" as aid or help. So what this scholar is saying is that, when God gives a man a job to do, he always gives him the power to do it.

You will find that true wherever you look in the Bible. God gave Moses the job of leading the people of Israel out of Egypt. When Moses began to beg off because he was not up to the task, God came to him then with his promise of aid: "Certainly I will be with thee." Here you have both "unconditional demand" and "final succor."

The fact that popular religion today soft-pedals the demand and overemphasizes the succor tends to make some people look askance at any promise of aid. Yet it is impossible to do the will of God without the help of God, and it is good to know that both belong to biblical faith. Whenever you are willing to say with our Lord, "I am come not to do my own will, but the will of him that sent me," then you have every right to say also, "God is my refuge and strength!" You can count upon it that God never sends you on a trip without filling your tank with gas, and as long as you are committed to the King's business, your gas will hold out.

This book is based on my pamphlet *More Power to You,* published by The Upper Room. It is written in the confidence that the power of God is available for us, and seeks to suggest certain practical ways by which we can "let" God help us.

JOHN A. REDHEAD

CONTENTS

ONE MAN'S STORY

This is a story that goes back eight years. It is the story of a man who found help from God when he needed it. There were three reasons for the need. First, not long before, I had turned the corner into the forties and discovered that physical fatigue is a problem to be reckoned with. Second, I had recently undergone a seven month's illness which took me in and out of hospitals four separate times and which culminated with an operation in Boston, all of which was severely depleting. Third, I had a job whose demands were becoming more and more strenuous, requiring from ten to fourteen hours a day. When you put these three things together, you find that you need a little extra strength from somewhere outside yourself. That strength was found, and this story is told with the hope that you may find it too.

It all began in the lobby of the beautiful Roanoke Hotel in Virginia. The ten days before had been busy ones. Beginning on a Sunday morning, I had spoken to the students at Northwestern University in Evanston, Illinois, and that night to the Chicago Sunday Evening Club. Back home in Greensboro, there was a full week of work waiting. On Thursday evening there was the annual congregational dinner to talk about financial needs for the next twelve months, and on Sunday morning the budget sermon, which takes more than the usual toll from a minister. After the service and a quick lunch a friend came by in his car, and we drove to Blacksburg in Virginia, where I spoke at a chapel dedication service. Leaving Blacksburg, we went on to Roanoke, where the churches had united in a city-wide preaching mission in which I had agreed to deliver eight addresses during the next three days. From Chicago to Greensboro to Blacksburg to Roanoke: it was a rather hectic week and a half.

On Wednesday evening of that week I found myself in the lobby of the Roanoke Hotel with a Baptist minister friend, Dr. George Heaton of Charlotte, North Carolina. We located two comfortable chairs and began talking shop, as two ministers will. I said, "George, when do you do your reading?" The hardest job a minister has is to find time to keep up his reading. I knew that Heaton must study a great deal, because he speaks on a variety of subjects, and every time he speaks he rings a bell. There is a vast difference between having to say something and having something to say. Heaton always has something to say, and so I asked, "Do you spend your mornings reading?" He answered that he did not. "Well," I said, "why?" And then he said, "Because I think I have found a way to help people get hold of the power of God, and I see a different person every fifteen minutes, for four hours a day, four days a week." Even I know enough arithmetic to know that that adds up to sixty-four people a week.

"Well," I said, "tell me what you do in those fifteen minutes." And he told me. He said he had the person sit in a comfortably relaxed position, then take several deep breaths, close his eyes, and think of some scene both pleasant and peaceful. When the sense of strain had been relaxed from his body and his mind, he suggested that his visitor make a mental image of himself kneeling near the front of his church. "Think of yourself as being alone there," he would say, "except for Christ. See him standing beside you and listen to him as he speaks some of his own recorded words."

I remembered that only a few weeks before Dr. Hornell Hart of Duke University had spoken in our church. It was the World Day of Prayer, and there were one thousand people present. He said he wanted to talk about prayer as a means to power. He asked the people if they believed in God and if they believed that the presence of God was as much available now as it was when Christ was alive in the flesh. By way of answer he asked them to raise their hands, and all hands went up. Then he put them through a set of exercises similar to those described by Heaton. I said, "George, what you are talking about sounds very much like what Dr. Hart did in our church the other day." And he answered: "Yes, it was from Dr. Hart that I learned what I do with my people."

Well, it sounded interesting, as you would find it interesting to hear any man tell of his work, but I paid no particular attention to anything he had said. What he was doing was teaching people to pray. I thought I had been praying for forty years, more or less, and I had never known anything you could call the power of God to come from it.

That was on Wednesday evening. On Thursday I went back to my home in Greensboro, and by nine o'clock on Friday morning I was in my study. As you can well imagine, the desk was covered with correspondence of the past four days, and it took me the whole morning to look after matters demanding attention. At noon I went home for lunch. I found I was eating alone, and the soup and the sandwich were finished in a few minutes.

Public speaking has always been an exhausting experience with me. I heard a man say once that after a sermon either the preacher or the people would be tired; and I've always felt it was up to me, as far as possible, to see to it that it was not the people. The physical and mental and spiritual drain which speaking imposes makes my body ache all over. Having been through a ten-day stretch for a total of thirteen addresses, you can well imagine what I felt like at that point, coupled with the fact that I had to go back to the study that afternoon and write a sermon for Sunday from beginning to end.

I have never quite understood why it was that before leaving for the church I went into the library and sat down in an easy chair, and put myself through the paces which Heaton had described. It was not that I expected anything to happen, because I did not. I took several deep breaths—feeling rather stupid all the while—tried to let the chair hold up my entire weight, thought of the most pleasant and peaceful scene I know, which to me is

, so I prepared a message called "The Pathway
" the substance of which will be found in Chap-
. I did my best to present a reasonable explana-
why it is essential to "let go" before you can
" and then I led the entire congregation along
that make up the pathway. There were some
he idea and who kept up the practice in private,
one reported having found new life.

pened that three years later I had the honor of
ing for Ralph Sockman on the National Radio
uring the summer months. I made bold to con-
same sort of "clinic in prayer" over the air.
the letters that came in response there was one
d in part:

r Dr. Redhead:
Sunday I was quite ill, was lying in bed, worried
ntic, because I think I had a slight stroke, and was
time unable to do anything for myself. I was trying
k of some way out, feeling very much like a rat in a
. . My cousin had put a small radio by my bed, I
use my body, but had very little co-ordination, and
tuned to NBC. I kept thinking, if I only knew *how*
y, and didn't feel like such a hypocrite when I try,
e I have felt that I had no right to ask a God I was
ven sure about for anything just because I was in
nity, when your broadcast started. Somehow your voice
rated the fog I was in. At any rate, you were broad-
g "The Pathway to Power." I do not claim to be
rted, that is just a word to me, but you did seem to
common sense explanation of how to pray.
the pent-up horror seemed to be leaving, there were
quiet tears, and as I was listening very intently, it

a golf fairway, and then I saw myself kneeling near the front of the church sanctuary with our Lord standing nearby, and then listened to him talk for a while in his own words which I recalled from memory.

After about fifteen minutes there came a most amazing experience. I felt the dull ache which is caused by nerve exhaustion begin to leave my body. It seemed to flow out through my finger tips, which tingled with that delightful sensation which you get sometimes after a rubdown in a health club. I felt completely refreshed all over and in a few minutes found myself saying to myself, "Why, this must be God, because this is new life and God is life." I felt for the first time in forty years that I had made direct contact with the God who is the life of all living things. After some thirty minutes I went on to the study, sat down at the typewriter, and wrote a full sermon without any sense of mental weariness whatsoever.

I began to wonder whether or not I had played some sort of psychological trick on myself. I did not speak of it to anyone until I could get back to my study and consult certain books which I knew could tell me whether it was a trick or whether it was true.

As soon as Sunday and its duties were over, I began to read—books like J. A. Hadfield's *Psychology of Power* and J. B. Pratt's *Religious Consciousness*. I was interested to find Hadfield saying this: "The fact that so many seek for power and do not receive it suggests that piety is not the only requisite for power." I found this man of science quoting the words of the prophet: "They that wait upon the Lord shall renew their strength."

He underscored the words "wait" and "renew" and indicated that there is a definite connection between the practice of repose and the reception of power. I remembered the emphasis which such men as Harry Emerson Fosdick and E. Stanley Jones had always placed upon what they called "relaxed receptivity" in preparation for prayer.

Then I recalled something which Leslie Weatherhead had written and found it in his book *The Transforming Friendship*. He says:

I have come home from some meetings thoroughly tired and disappointed and disillusioned. . . . I was too tired to pray, too tired to stir up any desire to pray, and then I tried an experiment. I relaxed the body and relaxed the mind, left, as it were, the door of the mind ajar. There was little more than a vague longing for the coming of the Friend, that Friend who understands. . . . And then something happened. The peace which is indescribable flooded the whole spirit; a hush which is ineffable quieted the mind. . . . The Friend came.

Once again, here was a man who had experimented with a certain method in prayer, and it worked.

Hadfield's statement quoted above began to haunt me: "Piety is not the only requisite for power." To piety, the willingness to pray, there must be added knowledge as to how to pray. I then began to understand why it is that we ministers so often fail our people. Too often we say to a person, "What you need is a good dose of prayer," without offering any help as to how to take the dose. And our prescription has been as in-

16

effective as that of some
patient, "What you need
taking out his little white
the patient is to take and

About that time there ap
of the *New York Times* a
book titled *Release from Ne*
headings looked interesting,
was written by a practicing
who offered practical suggest
seemed to me he had someth
to achieve that "relaxed rece
Bible places such importanc
Lord." I learned much from h
the necessity of a proper m
through prayer.

The more I thought about th
in the Bible, and the more I
science have to say, the more I
the experience of new life whic
day in the library is supposed to
ence of every believing Christian
logical trick. It was, after all, tru
my wife, who tried the method
She gave it the name "CS" for ci
the "siesta" has taken on new m
She said that her only difficulty
enough Bible verses, so she devi
Affirmations" which makes it as
twenty-six of these statements.

I felt that our people ought to k

had foun
to Power
ter Thre
tion as t
"let Goc
the step
who got
and eac

It ha
substitu
Pulpit
duct th
Among
that sa

My de
Last
and fr
at tha
to thi
trap.
could
it was
to pr
becau
not e
extre
pene
casti
conu
give

A
som

seemed that all my tenseness and some of my worry left me, and I got for that brief time perhaps a glimpse of what is called faith, and felt as though there might be a God who cared about the very imperfect people he had caused to be born. I couldn't *hold* the feeling, but even the short glimpse was heartening.

The letter goes on to report an improvement in physical condition, but that is not the point. The important thing is that, even over the air, God had come to a despairing, almost unbelieving mind with new heart and new hope. "I kept thinking, if I only knew *how* to pray." When that was given, new life came.

The "method" seems to work whether given in public worship or over the air, but the greatest satisfaction has come in private conference. Every minister who is alert to the needs of his people and aware of the resources of his faith has his hands full in personal counseling. We have been told from of old that "all our needs can be met in God" and that God answers our prayers in one of two ways: either he removes the "thorn" or the "cup" when we ask him or, if not, he gives us the strength to live with it. But how to get hold of that strength? Any honest minister hates himself for saying to a beleaguered man or woman: If only you have "faith," if only you will "pray," you will find help. But how? How to make faith work and how to find power in prayer? The satisfaction of being able to put into a man's hands a handle that he can take hold of, and by means of which he can throw his religion into gear and set it moving, has been inestimable.

19

Let me tell you about one experience out of many that have been mine over the years. On a certain weekday when I arrived at my study at nine in the morning, there was a young man in his middle thirties waiting to talk. He had a problem that had caused great concern to himself and his wife and because of which they had not had much sleep for several nights. We put our minds to his need as best we could and found some light for his problem. There was nothing more we could do at the moment, because the problem was such that only time could tell whether our suggested solution was the correct one.

In other years I would have told him good-by at that point and wished him well. But in the light of the experience described in these pages I found myself saying to him, "Bill, I can tell you are pretty close to the margin of your reserve strength; and if you have time, I would like to pass on to you something which has helped me."

He said he would gladly take time and so went through the exercises described by Dr. Heaton. We closed our eyes and thought of our chairs as holding up our entire weight. We talked to the muscle centers of our bodies, taking a number of deep breaths as we did so, to relax physical strain. Then we released the tension of our minds. Following that, we made a mental image of being in the church, alone with Christ, and listened to him talk.

After a total of about ten minutes I said "Amen." My friend sat quietly in silence for some seconds. I could see that the strained look on his face was gone and then he said, "I want to make a strange request."

"What is it?" I asked.

He replied, "I have felt closer to God in these few minutes than I ever have in my life, and I would like to nail down this experience by taking Communion with you."

"Well," I said, "I would be glad to do so, but I do not have the elements here."

"Oh!" he answered, "just plain water will do."

Fortunately in my desk was an individual Communion set, so I filled two cups with water. The only "bread" I could find was a little throat disk such as every public speaker keeps around. I broke it in two and put it on the plate, and there the two of us had our Communion.

When it was over, he said he would like to bring his wife back the next day. "As you know," he said, "we have several small children, and the job of looking after them is fatiguing. I think this sort of thing would help Jane too."

They came back the next day, and we practiced our "C.S." together, and then they left. Three days later they were back again. When I saw them, I was afraid the original problem had broken loose again, but I was pleasantly surprised. What they came to say was this: "You know what a heavy strain we have been under for these few days, but we have come to tell you that we are really thankful for our problem because it has been the means of helping us to find the strength of God in our daily living."

I think this experience was the most dramatic of the

results I have seen, but over the past years there have been many others who have found the help they needed in God. Long years ago the psalmist sang, "The Lord is the strength of my life." I used to wonder just exactly what he meant. Now I know. The following pages are written in order that you may know too.

CHAPTER TWO

THE SECRET AND THE SOURCE

In the last chapter I described the experience of one person who learned something of the power of God in daily living. The more I have thought about the experience, the more I have become convinced that the need of most of us centers right there. One morning our maid came to work looking all down in the mouth. My wife said to her, "Ruth, what is the matter?"

Her answer is one you cannot forget. "I don't know, Mrs. Redhead; I guess I'm just 'lergikin up to a nervous breakdown.' "

Everyone who has had the experience of trying to get into a hospital knows how full they are, and it has been said so often that now even the man in the street knows that every other hospital bed in the United States is occupied by someone whose illness is caused by something other than a physical malady. Legion is the name of those who have found themselves "lergikin up to a nervous breakdown."

Some years ago three people whom I had never seen before came to my study in the same week. The only reason I remember them is that each had the same story to tell: he had gone to pieces, been forced to give up his work, sought medical aid, discovered he needed something more than doctors can give, and had gone to a minister in search of the power of God. They all came from another town, and I have not seen them since. I am afraid I was not able to help them very much because they came in the days "B.C.S."—before I had any personal knowledge of the strength of God available in creative silence.

But it was different in the case of one married couple. A mutual friend brought one of them to my study. She and her husband were having a difficult time getting on, and she had been forced to see a psychiatrist. There were suspicions and accusations, and a bad time all the way around. Neither one was a member of a local church, and one had never made any profession of faith. Many were the half hours we spent practicing together the presence of God, and he did not let us down. She found the strength she needed to live with her problem. Then the thing happened that so often happens: God worked such a change in her life that it was noticeable at home. Her husband wanted to know how it happened, and she told him. Altogether on his own he came to say this: "My wife has found something that I want. Can you help me find it?" We went "into the silence" together, and God came to meet us, and now their home is a happy one and both are active members of a local church. I verily believe it was the power of God that saved that marriage, and I know God was able to get to these two people because they found the key that unlocked the door and let him in.

There is no need to emphasize further the need. You can look around you, and you can look within yourself, and you will see on every hand a need of the power of God. When you grow tired from your tasks and fatigue sets you on edge, how would you like to plug in on new power? When your sense of inadequacy makes you feel inferior to your responsibilities and you have that sickening sense of being unequal to what is expected of you, how would you like to know there is a power that can make you adequate? When you face a moral choice, knowing that failure to do the right thing will make you hate yourself, how would you like to believe that there is outside help to get you over the hump? When you have a decision to make and somehow cannot seem to get the right answer, how would you like to have a higher Wisdom "direct thy paths"? When you seek peace for yourself and there seems to be no peace, how would you like to find the "peace of God, which passeth all understanding"? When your tendency is to make mountains out of molehills, how would you like to be able to turn your mountains into molehills? To believe that the same boundless energy that makes the sun to shine and the trees to grow and the flowers to blossom is available to you, and to be able to get up each morning and face the day knowing that whatever you have to do you can do, is all that many of us would ask of God. Jesus says you can believe that, for "you shall receive power."

Every student of language knows that this word "power" comes from the Greek *dunamis,* which gives us our English word "dynamite." So what Jesus is saying in effect is this: You shall receive dynamite when the Holy Spirit is come upon you. Dynamite is stored-up energy, and the promise is that we shall receive such energy and strength and ability.

Another interesting word in this sentence is the word "receive." "But you shall receive power when the Holy Spirit has come upon you." (R.S.V.) That suggests that power is not something which is manufactured within us but something that is released through us. And it ties in with a truth that we see at work all around us—namely, that the secret of power lies in the principle of released energy.

By all odds the most dramatic illustration of this truth is atomic fission. Look at an ordinary lump of uranium ore and you will see nothing but that. Yet when a scientist takes that lump of ore into his laboratory, he releases energy sufficient to shake the world. So much so that one scientist took an ordinary cardboard railroad ticket from his pocket and said to a friend: "There is enough energy in that to drive an express train ten thousand miles." Then he added: "We'll tackle sand next, just ordinary sand; and in two handfuls of sand there is enough energy to supply all the basic power needs of the United States for the next two or three years." The secret of power from the atom lies in the principle of released energy.

The same thing is true of the tree in your yard or the rosebush in your garden. It does not make the power by which it grows. It lives by chemical assimilation through its roots and leaves of the energies of sunlight and plant food.

The same fact is true of your body. It is not self-contained, and it does not live by itself. It absorbs its lifegiving power by appropriating energy from sunshine and air and food. It exists on the principle of released energy.

Harry Emerson Fosdick has reminded us that it would be strange indeed if a principle that operates everywhere else did not hold good also when moved up to the level of our spirits. Looking at the secret of power in all other forms of being, we can expect that as human beings needing personal power this same principle will work for us.

The fascinating fact is that those who know best tell us that such is actually the case. When I went back to J. A. Hadfield's book *The Psychology of Power,* I found that he has coined two figures of speech. He says that you can see yourself in relation to the power question either as a reservoir or as a channel. If you think of yourself as a reservoir, then you see yourself as containing just so much strength and no more. You can think of yourself as getting your energy from the food you eat and the air you breathe, and it is strictly limited in amount. When you work hard, your energy runs low, so your tendency is to save yourself as much as possible, lest the reservoir go empty. But if you wish, you can become not a reservoir but a channel through which strength can flow. "The way to power, therefore," says Hadfield, "is not to harbour our resources and store up our strength by inactivity, but to find the way to tap the resources of power at our disposal, so that they may flood our life and fill us with energy." [1]

[1] Used by permission of St. Martin's Press.

These are the words of a medical specialist, which you have a right to believe in perfect intellectual honesty; but if you still doubt, you can try a simple experiment. When you come home from the office, you are usually so tired you cannot put one foot in front of the other. Suppose when you get home tomorrow, your wife asks you to mow the lawn. The mere thought of cutting the grass is enough to put you in bed, and you beg off. "Some other time, darling; today has been one of those days." But a few minutes later along comes a friend who asks you to join him for a few holes of golf. In a flash your fatigue takes wings and flies away; and when you come back after walking nine holes, you are talking about how good it is to get a little exercise! "You shall *receive* power," said Jesus. "Life is a channel, and strength comes from the principle of released energy."

But where does it come from? It comes from the source of all power—in the atom, in the plant, in your body—from God himself. "You shall receive power," said Jesus, "when the Holy Spirit has come upon you." The secret of power lies in the principle of released energy, and the source of power is God.

Many of you have read *Letters to Young Churches* and *The Gospels* as translated by J. B. Phillips of England. He has a translation of the book of Acts that he calls the *Young Church in Action*. In the preface he says this:

We in the modern church have unquestionably *lost* something. . . . We cannot help looking wistfully at the sheer spiritual power of the minute young Church. . . . People are unquestionably being changed at the root of their being: cowards become heroes; sinners are transformed; fear, greed, envy and pride are expelled by a flood of something over and above normal human experience.

And they go out to meet whatever the day calls for with a "gay and generous courage." That "something over and above normal human experience" is nothing more than the power of God promised by Jesus, and I believe it is available for his people today as it was then.

You find it wherever you look in the Bible. The psalmist says of the divine shepherd: "He restoreth my soul"—that is, God gives me new life, new strength, new power; he winds me up when I run down inside. You find the prophet saying: "They that wait upon the Lord shall renew their strength." You find a man named Paul in the New Testament saying: We are "strengthened with might by [God's] Spirit in the inner man." You find that same apostle putting it like this: "I can do all things through Christ which strengtheneth me." In contrast to our own powerlessness that makes us feel inadequate and leads us to say in the face of any responsibility, "I can't," Paul steps out saying, "I can." Yet he sees his power as something not self-produced but assimilated by the principle of released power. I can because he can, and because through him I am able. And the source of that power is unmistakable: It is God, who has come close in Christ.

You find this truth not only in the Bible but in books on science. Here is this same Hadfield, who puts it this way:

Speaking as a student of psychotherapy, who, as such, has no concern with theology, I am convinced that the Christian religion is one of the most potent influences that we possess for producing that harmony and peace of mind and that confidence of soul which is needed to bring health and power to a large proportion of nervous patients. In some cases I have attempted to cure nervous patients . . . but without success until I have linked . . . on to that faith in the power of God which is the substance of the Christian's confidence and hope. Then the patient has become strong.[2]

Hearing that from a doctor, you can better believe that a minister whom I know is working in the realm of fact when he lists the prayer meeting in his church bulletin not as prayer meeting but as an "hour of power."

The experience of the disciples, described by J. B. Phillips, suggests a further fact. The power they possessed was, as we have seen, released power. All of a sudden a group of men, who heretofore had been ordinary human beings, became literally "live wires." It was evident they had "received" something. More than that, this new power came from God. It was something beyond human experience, and they recognized that it was by the power of the Holy Spirit that they worked their miracles. But furthermore, it was conditional power. They had heard the call of their Lord to follow him, and they had committed themselves to the business of being his witnesses "in Jerusalem, and in all Judaea, and in Samaria, and unto the uttermost part of the

[2] *Ibid.*

earth." So it would seem that in addition to the secret, which is released power, and to the source, which is God himself, there is the condition of commitment. If you wish to let God help you, you must submit yourself to his will and commit yourself to his work.

That seems to make sense. Emerson said once that the "power of the Gulf Stream will flow through a straw if the straw be placed parallel to the Gulf Stream." The power of God will flow through your life when you put your life in line with the will of God. It has been estimated that 95 per cent of the energy it takes to grow a crop of wheat comes from the universe, and the other 5 per cent from the farmer. The power of electricity has been present in the world from the beginning of time, but only when Benjamin Franklin sent his kite into the air did he bring it down. God takes the initiative and offers his power for personal living today, but it is available only when you meet his laws, one of which is this: Get in step with his will and commit yourself to what that requires.

It is everlastingly true that when God comes to meet a man he comes, as Herbert H. Farmer says, in the two ways of "unconditional demand" and "final succor"; and if a man wishes the "succor," he must meet the "demand."

It was certainly true in the experience of Jesus. God came to him with a demand that he could not shake off, it was so unconditional that in the end it cost him his life, and yet all the way through he found a strength to sustain him. One day, you remember, he was sitting by a well. He was on his way from Judea to Galilee, and John says he was weary from the journey. His men had gone off to get something to eat, and while he sat by the well, a woman came to draw water. The two of them fell to talking, and just as she left, his men returned. When they urged him to eat, he replied, "I have meat to eat that ye know not of." They thought someone else had given him something to eat, and when he heard them talking among themselves about it, he said, "My meat is to do the will of him that sent me, and to finish his work." He affirms the fact that in meeting the condition of what he believes to be the will of his Father for his life, he finds an inner sustenance that gives him energy and makes him strong.

It is even so today. Theodore Ferris of Trinity Church, Boston, told his congregation how he learned this truth. He said:

It was the summer before I went to my first work as the rector of Emmanuel Church in Baltimore. I was twenty-eight years old; I had practically no experience; it was a big, city church; and I was frightened. That whole summer during my vacation in Nova Scotia, I was in a state of uncontrolled anxiety, which other people may not have recognized, but which destroyed all my pleasure, and prevented any real recreation. Finally, one night when I couldn't go to sleep, I heard a few simple words. I didn't hear any voice, but the words were just as definite as though they had been written on my mind forever. And these were the words: "I will give you strength when you get there." All my anxieties relaxed and were relieved and, when I got there, He did give me the strength.

It will be something of a red-letter day in your experience when you are able to put together these two facts of demand and succor. To many people God is no more than a taskmaster who says, "Thou shalt do this," or "Thou shalt endure that." They feel that the only place he touches their life is in placing upon it some job to be done or some burden to be borne. But it's good news to know that, whenever he gives you a job to do, he gives you also the power to do it. And so when you see the truth in its full light, you put it like this: "God is more than my taskmaster; he is also the strength of my life."

Long ago I read a story whose truth has since been proved in experience. In one of the tidal rivers of New York the building of a bridge was interrupted by a tramp ship being sunk in the river's bottom. Divers put chains about the sunken ship and fastened the chains to tugboats, and they puffed and pulled and nothing happened. Then a young student, fresh from technical school, asked for a chance to try. The old engineer looked down his nose at this young upstart and asked, "What will *you* do it with?"

"I'm going to try the flatboats in which we brought the granite from Vermont," he answered.

So when the tide went out, the flatboats were chained to the derelict. Then the Atlantic began to come in. The tides put their shoulders underneath the flatboats and lifted—lifted until the sunken ship had to come. When the young man got in step with the "will" of the universe, he was able to harness its power to his task.

A golfer reached the age and station when he had to put on bifocals. His doctor dreaded breaking the bad news because he knew what the new lenses would do to his patient's game. Finally he could wait no longer, and having equipped his patient he gave him a wide berth. One day they met face to face, and the doctor braced himself for the storm he knew would break. He was pleasantly surprised, however, when his patient said to him: "Doc, I want to tell you about those new glasses. They're the best thing that's ever happened to my game. Why, they've cut six strokes off my score."

The doctor was much relieved and said, "That's fine; tell me about it."

"Well," said the golfer, "I take my driver and I look down and see two balls, a big one and a little one. I swing at the big one and can't miss it; it goes right down the fairway. Then I take my iron and look down, and I see two balls, a big one and a little one. I swing at the big one and can't miss it; it goes right up on the green. Then I look down again and see two balls, a big one and a little one; I look over by the pin and see two cups, a big one and a little one. So I just putt the little ball into the big cup, and it goes in every time."

Much depends upon the matter of perspective. Many people would be better off if they had the bifocals of faith—if they could see that they are not going it alone; that, standing there, is Another and that his word is this: "My grace is sufficient for thee."

Here is a man who put it like this: "When I pray, I feel as if I am plugging in on the power of the universe." Would you like to find it that way? We move on then to think about the kind of prayer that is a pathway to power.

CHAPTER THREE

THE PATHWAY TO POWER

In the last chapter I spoke of the need for power as the central need that so many face. We noticed that the secret of power lies in the principle of released energy and that the source of power is God. In this chapter we go on to think about the steps on our part that are essential in making contact with that Source.

In the first chapter of the book of Acts our Lord said to his men: "You shall receive power when the Holy Spirit has come upon you" (R.S.V.). In the second chapter the promise is fulfilled in a Pentecost of power. Students of the Bible have studied these verses and have told us that the conditions for power are things like prayer, and expectancy, and submission to the will of God, and faith. Some of us have done our best to meet these conditions, and nothing has happened. Instead of receiving the power that was promised, we have remained in the shallows of our weakness.

Yet when we have gone back to look at the first condition in the light of certain truth that our students of human nature have given us today, we have found the secret of contact with the Source. During the forty days between the Resurrection and the Ascension, Jesus met with his men and "commanded them that they should not depart from Jerusalem, but wait for the promise of the Father." After he was lifted up out of their sight, they went back to the city from Olivet and assembled in the upper room. Then the Bible says: "All these with one accord devoted themselves to prayer" (R.S.V.). For ten days they prayed and they waited, and they waited and they prayed, and then they received the power of the Spirit. It would seem that the prayer that waits before God is the means of power.

In the light of that fact it is interesting to learn what a man of science in our time has to say. J. A. Hadfield made a study of the power question from the standpoint of the workings of human nature, and then he wrote this: "I need only indicate the close connection between restfulness of mind, so essential to the cure of nervous ills, and that characteristic of religious devotion." [1] It is in this place that he quotes the word of the prophet, "They that wait upon the Lord shall renew their strength," and that he underscores the words "wait" and "renew." He believes there is a direct connection between the practice of the quiet mind that "waits on the Lord" and the renewal of strength.

In the light of that fact it is evident that, if we wish to get our hands on the power of God, we must travel the way to power; and on that pathway there are two steps: letting go and letting God.

What do I mean by letting go? I mean the practice of a prescribed set of exercises calculated to induce a condition of relaxed receptivity.

Students of human nature have helped us to under-

[1] *Ibid.*

stand why that step is necessary as a condition for the reception of power. Here in your arm is the muscle that gets tired, and here is God, the source of power. But your muscle is a physical thing, and God is a spirit. How can you plug in on God, as you put an electric plug in its socket? In this way: Your muscle is controlled by a nerve, and the nerve is connected with your brain, and your brain is controlled by your mind, and your mind can make contact with God. Why is it then that you ever lack strength if you have that connection with such a dynamo?

The answer is that there is a short circuit along the line. That short circuit is caused by something that we call tension. Running throughout your body there is a network of little electric wires that we call nerves. Whenever you are worried or frightened or frustrated, whenever you face a problem you cannot solve, something called tension builds up in these wires. Tension is said to be the characteristic disease of our time. If a passenger missed the stagecoach in the old days, so the story goes, he would wait patiently until the next one the following week; but now if a man misses one section of a revolving door, he has a nervous breakdown. My father did his courting by driving the fourteen miles from his plantation to my mother's home in a horse and buggy. I have heard him say that many a time, on leaving there late at night, he would throw the reins over the dashboard and go to sleep, and when he waked, the horse would be standing in front of his own gate. Try driving an automobile in that "relaxed" condition and see what would happen! It might be that our mechanized age has something to do with our increased tension. Anyway, you can watch the look on the face of a person driving a horse and buggy and of the chauffeur of a car and see the difference!

The reason why so many people are nervous today is not that we have nerves; we could not get along without those; it is because we allow so much tension to build up within them that it causes a short circuit of power. The figure of the electric wire fits the truth given us by Hadfield, namely, that our life is a channel. But if a channel is blocked, there can be no flow of power. And tension is the thing that causes the block. How then can we get rid of it?

Those who know tell us that, just as you can neutralize an electric charge in a wire by grounding it, so you can release tension in your nerves by relaxation. The first time I had any sense of the power of God flooding my being, it came, you remember, after I had practiced a set of exercises calculated to relax the body. I wondered why a physical thing like bodily relaxation had anything to do with a spiritual experience like prayer. The answer I found was that tension of the mind is built up and stored in physical parts of the body like nerves, and the work of releasing tension must begin there. As a matter of fact, you may be carrying about within your nerves now tensions that have been building up across the years, and you will never get rid of them until you learn to relax.

Ever since this truth was made plain to my mind, I have discovered that all teachers of the art of prayer begin with a first step of relaxed receptivity. The word "relaxation" is not in good standing just now with some religious thinkers; but do what you will with the word, the meaning for which it stands is essential in the practice of prayer as a means to power.

Listen to Henry N. Wieman, writing in 1929 in his book *Methods of Private Religious Living:* "The first step in the act of worship is to relax and to become aware of that upon which you are dependent." [2]

Listen to Georgia Harkness in her *Prayer and the Common Life:*

There seem to me four essential steps. The first is *relaxation.* This means one ought to get as comfortable as possible without going to sleep. . . . For this reason it is usually better to sit in a comfortable chair or lie on one's back, with the weight as evenly distributed as possible. Then relax the body's tense muscles. Most people do not realize how tense they are until they stop to think of it. This is a good time to think of it, and physical relaxation is a good introduction to spiritual composure. . . . With the body as relaxed as you can make it, relax the mind.

Listen, too, to Nels F. S. Ferré in his little book *Strengthening the Spiritual Life:*

The first rule we all need to learn [in the practice of prayer] is relaxation. . . . We have to let go. . . . It is better . . . to lie in bed while praying in order to relax than to kneel in stiff discomfort on a stone floor. . . . Comfortable sitting or lying I believe to be important aids to relaxed prayer. . . . Conscious relaxation of wrists, ankles, and neck

[2] Copyright 1929 and used by permission of The Macmillan Co.

also help in the physical preparation. . . . In any case, bodily relaxation I believe to be of utmost importance for effective prayer.

Here is a man of large responsibility in the business world. A friend asked why it was that so many people in like positions had breakdowns and he never seemed to be even near the edge of one. He said, "Just two words." When his friend wanted to know what he meant, he told this story. He said that when he was a young man he was out swimming with a girl who was an expert and that he became frightened when he thought how deep the water was and was afraid of going down. When the girl saw what was happening, she did not get flustered but said calmly, "Frank, float." He said he took her advice and came out safely.

Swimmers know that when you float you have a sense of power not your own holding you up, but that in order to float you must be completely relaxed. You must let go. When you do that, you can stay on top and keep your head above water for as long as you like.

It is not otherwise in this business of prayer. You can have a sense of power not your own holding you up and carrying you on, but in order to have it you must first let go and by doing so neutralize the tension that is blocking the channel to power. First, then, let go.

You are ready now for the second step along the pathway to power. Not only do you "wait," but you "wait on the Lord." Not only do you "let go," but you "let God." "Letting God" means that, after you have spent from five to ten minutes in inducing that state of relaxed receptivity, your prayer takes the form of affirming your faith that the "Lord is the strength of [your] life."

The Bible has been described as "pages of power." It is literally that. There is an amazing power in words, because of a law of human nature that tells us that, once an idea has been accepted by your mind, it tends to come true in your life. The only way you can grow strong from the food on your table is to open your mouth and receive and appropriate it. The only way you can grow strong from the power of God is the same: to open your mind and receive and appropriate the bread of life by the prayer of affirmation.

So what you need to do is to go through your Bible and select certain verses that affirm the power of God to make you strong. "The Lord is the strength of my life." "He restoreth my soul." We are "strengthened with might by [God's] Spirit in the inner man." "In him who strengthens me, I am able for anything." Find at least twenty or twenty-five and commit them to memory. Then when you have become relaxed and have opened the channel by the release of tension, you are ready to receive the strength of God that comes through your prayer that affirms his power to make you strong.

Here is a picture of this truth. Muriel Lester of London has written a little pamphlet called *Ways of Praying* in which she has a section on "The Prayer of Relaxation." In that section she tells this story:

I had been living on my nerves for a year or so without knowing it, due to a series of calamities that had battered

41

upon my family. Do you remember the old phrase used in the push bike era? When the tire went flat, one was said to be "riding on the rims." It was bad for the tires, and it seemed to me that living on one's nerves was like that, making one jagged, ragged. I felt like a piece of overstrong elastic, or a bit of frayed string, or yesterday's lettuce. The elastic cannot regain its resilience, nor the string its firmness, but the lettuce can recover its vigor, if it is plunged into water, because it is alive. And I knew that I could recover my freshness both physically and spiritually as soon as I could become receptive to the all-pervading power of God. So for an hour each day I set myself the definite task of gaining renewal of vitality from God through relaxation.

I stretched myself out on my back, my weight concentrated on the nerve plexus at the back of the waist. Then I relaxed my muscles. . . . I loosened my finger muscles and spread out my hand as though it were the model for an artist; made the whole arm relaxed, loosened, so that when it was raised, it fell heavy and inert in whichever direction it was tossed, like a sleeping child's; then the same with the toes and the feet; then the same, a much harder task, with the face muscles. I discovered that when the face muscles are relaxed one automatically smiles, hence the smile on the face of the dead, when the nerves are functioning no longer. . . . But this time, I would find the hand and finger muscles all taut again, and they had to be again relaxed, then the feet, then the face. It would take perhaps fifteen minutes to get really relaxed all over, then one could begin the cure. . . .

The tiredness was gradually transformed into deep restfulness, until I could say to myself, not in words, but in my mind, "With every breath I draw, I am breathing in the very breath of God." These lifegiving exercises I continued indefinitely until my whole being seemed to be enveloped by a great sense of peace and I felt that the prayer of relaxation was like a good, strong raft on which men could ride over the deepest and blackest of waters in perfect safety and delight.

There is the story of the pathway to power, described by one who traveled it and who came back to say that it works. Let go and let God, and then you will know that "they that wait upon the Lord shall renew their strength."

If now you would like to "plug in on the power of God," suppose you read over several times from here to the end of the chapter, so that you may follow the suggestions with your eyes closed.

First of all find a place where you may be quiet. You may sit or lie down, as you choose. If you use a chair, sit with your back against it and put your feet flat on the floor. If you lie down, put a pillow under your knees, as nurses teach you to do in the hospital. Then take the corners of the pillow under your head and pull them up over your shoulders. You will find, as Dr. Fink says, that such a posture is most conducive to relaxation. Now make a fist out of both hands and raise your toes toward your head. These actions exercise the muscles in your hands and legs and help the nerves to relax. Close your eyes, bend your head forward slightly, and put your tongue between your teeth. Next, release the pressure in the grip of your hands and the muscles of your legs.

Now talk to the muscle centers of your body. Begin with the muscles in your scalp. Take a deep breath and as you exhale, say to these muscles, let go, let go, let go more. Think of the muscles in your eyes. Take a deep breath and as you exhale, say to these muscles, let go, let go, let go more. Think of the muscles across your forehead and around your eyes and in your cheeks and around your mouth. Take a deep breath and as you exhale, say to these muscles, let go, let go, let go more. Think of the muscles in your neck and across your shoulders—driving an automobile makes you very tense in these places. Take a deep breath and as you exhale, say to these muscles, let go, let go, let go more.

In this manner go down the list one by one and relax all the major muscle centers in your body: your chest, your back, your arms (upper arm, forearm, wrist, palm), your fingers (thumb, forefinger, middle finger, fourth finger, little finger), your legs (thigh, calf, ankle, foot, toes). It will take possibly ten minutes to cover the ground and maybe several weeks of practice in order to learn to relax completely.

Having relaxed your body, you are ready to do the same for your mind. Think of some scene that is pleasant and peaceful. For the psalmist it was green pastures and still waters. Think of lying down on the green grass on a lazy summer afternoon, as you did many a time when you were a child. See yourself sitting on the shore of a beautiful lake where the water is calm and quiet. So, says the psalmist, "he restoreth my soul," giving me new life. Think of your right hand as a wet leaf lying limp on a log. Think of your left hand as a damp dishcloth hanging limp on a line. Think of yourself as a kitten lying on the hearth, as a child asleep on a bed. Make a mental image of a basketball as it is being deflated, of a kite in the air when the string is cut, and see it collapse. Think of the leaves in the autumn falling from the trees—falling, falling, falling. Think of yourself as a snow man when the sun comes out and feel yourself melting, melting, melting. Think of being at the beach in the summer and see yourself floating on top of the water—floating, floating, floating. You feel a power not your own holding you up, so it is that "underneath are the everlasting arms."

Now you are being relaxed physically and mentally, and the tension in your body and your mind is being released. Now the channel is open, and you are ready to receive the strength that comes from God.

Now think of yourself as being in your church, sitting near the front. You are all alone and you are refreshed by the quiet of the place and the beauty of the stained glass. Then the door near the pulpit opens, and Someone comes in. You look up and notice that it is our Lord himself, and you are impressed by the peace and calm of his countenance. He walks over to where you sit and begins to talk to you, and his voice is friendly and encouraging.

"Come unto me, all ye that labour and are heavy laden, and I will give you rest." Rest, he says; and the very sound of the word is like music to your ears, for you are restless so much of the time. "I will give you rest." He speaks again and he says, "In quietness and in confidence shall be your strength": in quietness, in

45

this attitude of relaxed receptivity, and in confidence: in the confident belief that the strength of God is available to you; "in quietness and in confidence shall be your strength." He speaks again and he says, "Be still, and know that I am God." Let go and let God. He speaks again and he says, "They that wait upon the Lord shall renew their strength": they who take time out of a busy day to grow still and be quiet (remember only a quiet pool can catch a reflection—"they that wait upon the Lord shall renew their strength." (There is no need to hurry to leave; he will stay and talk to you as long as you wish.)

Now you are beginning to feel new life flood your veins. Now you know what the psalmist meant when he said, "The Lord is the strength of my life." Now you know what our Lord meant when he said, "You shall receive power when the Holy Spirit has come upon you." Now you know what it means to be strengthened with might by God's spirit in the inner man. Now you are almost able to say with the apostle, "I can do all things through Christ which strengtheneth me." Now the strength of God is yours, and you are strong in the strength of God.

And now you will want to talk to him in some such way as this: "Lord, I thank thee that thou didst promise that thou wouldst never go away, that thou wouldst be with us every day. I thank thee that thou art as close to me as my own thoughts and I have only to stop and grow quiet and think of thee and thou art here, and that from thy presence I can rise strong and able to do all that I have to do. Now the peace of God is mine

because I have found my way into the power of God.
And I thank thee.

"Drop Thy still dews of quietness,
Till all our strivings cease;
Take from our souls the strain and stress,
And let our ordered lives confess
The beauty of Thy peace. Amen."

CHAPTER FOUR

POWER FOR YOUR BODY

In the last chapter the pathway to power was described as consisting of two steps: first, letting go and, second, letting God. Now we begin to think of some of the ways in which the power that comes can be experienced in daily living.

Many years ago I went with some friends to a conference in Massachusetts. When the train from New York stopped at Northfield, we noticed a man get off at the station and board the bus for the hotel. He was of slight build, bareheaded, and seemed so young. We supposed he was a delegate on his way to attend the conference. You can imagine our surprise when that young man walked up on the platform that evening and was introduced as the Rev. Dr. James S. Stewart, widely known author and preacher of Scotland.

We liked so much what he had to say that we began looking around for books he had written. The most recent was a volume titled *The Gates of New Life*. All the chapters are excellent, but there is one that has intrigued me ever since. It is called "The Fellowship of the Spirit" and is a study of the lives of the men in the book of Acts. One thing it says is that, when these men were filled with the Spirit, they acquired a new power. He described that power as something

48

that was active on physical and mental and moral and spiritual levels. For some eight years I failed to understand what he meant, and then after the experience presented in Chapter One I began to see his meaning from the inside.

Long years ago I read an article on prayer by Dr. Alexis Carrel, fellow of the American College of Surgeons. What he wrote seemed so far beyond anything I had ever experienced that I put it aside. More lately, however, I have gone back to reread his statement, and I found him saying this: "The influence of prayer on the human mind and body is as demonstrable as that of secreting glands. Its results can be measured in terms of increased physical buoyancy, greater intellectual vigor, moral stamina, and deeper understanding of the realities underlying human relationships."

Once again we find a student of the Bible and a man of science saying the same thing about the power of God as power for living. They agree in the fact that it can be known in the areas of physical and mental and moral and spiritual experience.

In this chapter we are concerned only with the first, with power for your body. It seems to me that the power of God received through prayer can have results for our bodies in two ways.

The first is in overcoming fatigue by providing an added physical buoyancy. James Stewart puts it like this: "Look at the men of the New Testament. Quite apart from their spiritual force, they were physically twice the men they had been before, tingling with an energy and a verve which they themselves formerly would not have believed possible, and carrying things through triumphantly which would once have broken them." [1]

The older we grow, the more we have to take into account this thing called fatigue. One week I happened to announce for our Sunday-night-forum topic an old African proverb that says, "Don't be tired tomorrow." To my surprise more people came that night than had come to any of the meetings in five years. I discovered there are more tired people in Greensboro than I had thought.

Listen in on the conversation of any group and you will discover what a big problem is fatigue. Everybody talks about how tired he is. The businessman's work piles so high at the office that he brings some of it home with him and so makes himself more tired. Instead of getting sympathy for having to work so hard, he only gets a proverb to the effect that while

> Man's work lasts till set of sun,
> Woman's work is never done.

He learns that instead of getting sympathy he is expected to give it.

Many of our problems in human relations find their cause right here in the emotional loss of self-control that comes from overfatigue. You will do things and say things when you are tired that you would never have done or said otherwise. A day at the office starts

[1] *The Gates of New Life.* Used by permission of Chas. Scribner's Sons and T. & T. Clark.

off beautifully because everybody is rested in the morning, but as the hours wear on and workers grow tired, tempers get thin and words begin to fly. At the end of the day the mother of young children begins to wonder if she has given birth to a brood of little hyenas. The truth is the children are not any more mischievous at supper than they were at breakfast, but fatigue has worn her patience thin.

I know a man who is organist in his church. He said he was to play for a wedding one day, and he and the groom were waiting behind the scenes for time to go into the church. The groom did not appear to be in his usual high spirits, and the organist asked him: "What's the matter, have you lost your ring?"

"No," said the groom, "I haven't lost my ring."

"Have you lost your best man?"

"No, I haven't lost my best man."

"Well," said the organist, "what is the matter?"

To which the groom replied with a long face and in a lugubrious voice: "I've lost my enthusiasm."

If you have lost your enthusiasm for your work and feel tired all the time, the chances are that your fatigue comes largely from tension. Many of us have jobs that require more work than the clock has time for. Consequently we are rushed all the time. When we get out of bed in the morning, we are already behind schedule, and we never catch up. We are like the little girl who said, "I feel in a hurry all over." It is not so much the work that wears us out as the worry, and the first cure for that worry lies in the quiet mind induced by relaxation.

The key to the understanding of that fact lies in the insight that we think with our bodies as well with our brains. William James defined an emotion for us as a "state of mind which is reflected by a sensible change in the body." The important thing there is that a state of mind is echoed in the tissues of the body. When you stop to think, you can see that truth as plain as the nose on your face. For example, if someone should walk up to you and insult you, you would get red in the face. Your emotion of anger is a state of mind that dilates the blood vessels in your cheeks and results in a sensible change in your body.

Knowing this plain fact of experience as you do, there is no mystery at all as to why a relaxed mind is medicine for your body. The reason is that a tense mind, one that is restless and overly active, running in circles like a merry-go-round, uses up your physical energy and makes you tired. You are like an automobile in which the motor is left running while it is standing still; let it stay that way long enough and it will run out of gas, even though it does not budge an inch. Sometimes when you wake up in the morning, you are just as tired as you were when you went to sleep. The reason is that you left your motor running. That deep mind of yours kept on working while you were asleep, and those same restless thoughts that fatigued you in the first place kept you from being refreshed in sleep.

It is interesting to find Isaiah talking about a strength that can help you to "mount up with wings as eagles; . . . run, and not be weary; and . . . walk, and not faint." If you wonder why the prophet's promise presents a climax in reverse, descending from winging to walking, the answer is that he is realistic. He knows what life is like. In our younger days we are robust in strength and feel that we can mount up with wings and fly; then as the years advance, we give up flying and are content with running; and finally, we slow down from running to a walk, and our problem comes to be how to walk and not faint. The prophet's answer is, as has been suggested, in two parts.

The first is this: "They that wait . . . shall renew their strength." Taking time out to grow quiet and be still, the practice of a relaxed receptivity that releases the tension and removes the restlessness of the mind, will have its own restoring power. Wilfred Funk, the man who makes dictionaries, picked out what to him were the ten most beautiful words in our language; and the one that he put at the top of the list was the word "tranquil." I wonder if a part of the reason for his selection is not the fact that the idea of tranquillity suggested by the word is so appealing and so much needed and so healing and life-giving to our jaded and fatigued spirits.

But Isaiah suggests that we shall find the strength we need not only by letting go but by letting God. "They that wait *upon the Lord* shall renew their strength." Believe it or not, you can measure in terms of pounds the difference in the physical strength of a man as it is controlled by ideas in his mind.

Our friend J. A. Hadfield says he conducted an experiment that proves such is possible. He asked three men to submit themselves to the test of mental suggestion on their strength by means of a gripping machine called a dynamometer. He had the three of them grip the machine with all their might in their normal waking condition, and their average strength in terms of pounds was 101. Then he hypnotized them, because under hypnosis the mind is more suggestible, and told them that they were weak. When their minds had accepted the idea of weakness, he had them grip the machine again, and their average strength had dropped to 29 pounds. Then while they were still under hypnosis, he told them that they were very strong. When their minds had accepted the idea of strength, he had them grip the machine again, and their average power had risen to 142 pounds. "In brief," says Hadfield, "when I suggested 'weakness,' the full flood of energy was checked and the men were capable of only one-third of their normal strength, whereas by suggestion of 'strength' latent powers were liberated and their normal strength increased by half as much again." [2]

You can see immediately the meaning this truth has for us in the practice of prayer as a means to power that overcomes fatigue. When once an idea is accepted by the deep mind, it tends to come true in your life, even to the point of physical strength that can be measured in pounds. So when you pray, you will first of all let go and release the tension that blocks the channel. Then you will let God by affirming over and over again the truth of your faith that "the Lord is the strength of my life." The same idea can be fed to

[2] *Op. cit.* Used by permission of St. Martin's Press.

the mind by means of many different verses that express the truth in various ways.

So much for the first of the ways by which the practice of the presence of God can provide power for the body. It overcomes fatigue. We move on now to a consideration of the second, which is health. The prayers of most of us include a request for health and strength. When you stop to think about it, these are the very gifts that await us at the end of the pathway to power.

Suppose we begin our study of the question of health by recalling an experience of his own that E. Stanley Jones has described for us in *The Christ of the Indian Road*. He says:

I was physically broken. The eight years of strain had brought on a nervous exhaustion and brain fatigue so that there were several collapses in India before I left for furlough. On board ship while speaking in a Sunday morning service there was another collapse. I took a year's furlough in America. On my way back to India I was holding evangelistic meetings among the university students of the Philippine Islands at Manila. Several hundreds of these Roman Catholic students professed conversion. But in the midst of the strain of the meetings my old trouble came back. There were several collapses. I went on to India with a deepening cloud over me. Here I was beginning a new term of service in this trying climate and beginning it—broken. . . .

I saw that unless I got help from somewhere I would have to give up my missionary career, go back to America and go to work on a farm to try to regain my health. It was one of my darkest hours. At that time I was in a meeting at Lucknow. While in prayer, not particularly thinking about myself, a Voice seemed to say, "Are you yourself ready for this work to which I have called you?" I replied: "No, Lord, I am done for. I have reached the end of my resources." The Voice replied, "If you will turn that over to me and not worry about it, I will take care of it." I quickly answered, "Lord, I close the bargain right here." A great peace settled into my heart and pervaded me. I knew it was done! Life—abundant Life—had taken possession of me. I was so lifted up that I scarcely touched the road as I quietly walked home that night. Every inch was holy ground. For days after that I hardly knew I had a body. I went through the days, working all day and far into the night, and came down to bedtime wondering why in the world I should ever go to bed at all, for there was not the slightest trace of tiredness of any kind. I seemed possessed by Life. . . .

Nine of the most strenuous years of my life have gone by since then, and the old trouble has never returned, and I have never had such health. But it was more than a physical Touch. I seemed to have tapped new Life for body, mind, and spirit. Life was on a permanently higher level. And I had done nothing but take it! [3]

Here is a man who claims to have found healing for his body through power from God. This story is a dramatic witness to truth and the kind of story a preacher would like to be able to tell from the pulpit. I was never able to use it until the last few years, however, because I had never seen anything like it and it could not sound convincing coming from me. Now I am prepared to believe it possible because I believe that the power of God is available to us in various

[3] Used by permission of Abingdon Press.

ways for physical health. The cure must have been effective for Jones, for after all these years he is still active.

Muriel Lester reports that she was cured from an overstrained heart through the prayer of relaxation. Nels Ferré says this: "The more I have prayed . . . the more I have discovered how God uses such means [physical techniques]; the actual result has been health and creative zest."

For many years the established churches have shown little interest in health, but now there is a general awakening of interest in the relation between religion and health of the body. To say the least, it is something worth thinking about when you find the *British Medical Journal* saying that "there is no tissue of the human body wholly removed from the influence of the spirit." I find myself in agreement with Dr. Cairns that "in the present state of knowledge for physical troubles, physical methods are the safest, quickest, and most efficient." Yet that does not rule out in any sense the power of God available for physical well-being.

Perhaps the wisest emphasis for the present is the prevention of illness that a practice of our faith can effect. E. Stanley Jones writes in his book *Mastery:*

An article in the *Reader's Digest* gives the theory that the basis of all diseases is what a doctor calls "stress." He became interested not in specific diseases but in the possible cause of all diseases—something that lay back of everything. And he fastened on stress. When one is under stress, the glands throw their secretions into the system to maintain the balance of the organism. But if the stress is long continued, then the defense mechanism breaks down; and the balance is not maintained. When that happens, disease may break out anywhere in the body; and that disease may be of various kinds. But the cause back of it all is stress. If that is true, then the maintenance of inner rest and poise is an absolute necessity for health.[4]

For a long time we divided a man into three compartments of body, mind, and spirit, and supposed that the three remained separate and had nothing to do with one another. But today we are learning that they are so closely akin that one catches the diseases of the other. Just as a splitting headache can keep you from thinking clearly, so can the poison of envy or resentment or fear make you physically ill. Doctors are aware of this fact and have developed a science known as psychosomatic medicine. "Psycho" means mind and "soma" means body, and psychosomatic medicine treats an illness of the body that has its origin in the mind. One doctor goes so far as to say that, if we Christians really believed and practiced the faith we profess, half our illnesses would drop off tomorrow morning. If the fruits of the Spirit are love and joy and peace, and if their opposites cause disease, then it is reasonable to suppose that the Spirit of God is a source of power for health.

I asked a doctor once if over a long period of time the practice of the quiet mind in religious devotion would not eliminate the necessity of shock treatments, and he said Yes, that the shock treatment is a drastic

[4] Used by permission of Abingdon Press.

method of untying knots that never would have developed had the patient known and practiced the calm confidence of religious faith.

If you wish new health and strength, go back now to the pathway of power and read again the detailed suggestions on the two steps. Once you have read them, practice them. Practice them until you have learned to relax both physically and mentally. Even though you are convinced of their reasonableness, they will do you no good unless you put them into operation. All the food on the table will not make you strong unless you eat it; neither will all the medicine in the drugstore make you well unless you take it. It is not without reason that prayer has been called the *"practice* of the presence of God." I like to think that, just as we take our physical food three times a day, so it ought to be with our spiritual food. Find five or ten minutes morning and evening, preferably just after you wake up and just before you go to sleep, and if possible in the middle of the day, to let go and let God.

Once you have found release from tension and have achieved a relaxed receptivity, then you are ready for the power of God to refresh and restore your body. Remember the two steps of visualization and verbalization. Make a mental image of yourself as being in the presence of Christ and listen to him as he talks to you. As you read your Bible, make your own list of verses that say the things you need to have said. In addition to your own selections you may wish to use some of the following, which have been classified by the late Charles R. Brown of Yale:

1. To Develop Strength

They that wait upon the Lord shall renew their strength. (Isa. 40:31.)

The Lord will give strength unto his people. . . . They go from strength to strength. (Ps. 29:11; 84:7.)

The Lord is the strength of my life; of whom shall I be afraid? (Ps. 27:1.)

I can do all things through Christ which strengtheneth me. (Phil. 4:13.)

2. To Induce Sleep

Come unto me, all ye that labour and are heavy laden, and I will give you rest. (Matt. 11:28.)

There remaineth therefore a rest to the people of God. (Heb. 4:9.)

I will both lay me down in peace, and sleep: for thou, Lord, only makest me dwell in safety. (Ps. 4:8.)

He giveth his beloved sleep. (Ps. 127:2.)

3. To Promote Healing

The leaves of the tree were for the healing of the nations. (Rev. 22:2.)

The Sun of righteousness [is risen] with healing in his wings. (Mal. 4:2.)

The prayer of faith shall save the sick. (Jas. 5:15.)

Who forgiveth all [my] iniquities; who healeth all [my] diseases. (Ps. 103.3.)

CHAPTER FIVE

POWER FOR YOUR MIND

Thanks to Mr. Edison one of the uses to which electric power is put is to give us light. Likewise, the power of God can be had as light for your mind.

Remember the word of James Stewart to the effect that, when the Spirit of God laid hold upon the men in the book of the Acts, one way in which that power was known was on the level of the mental. And recall again the statement of the scientist Alexis Carrel: "The influence of prayer on the human mind . . . is as demonstrable as that of secreting glands. Its results can be measured in terms of . . . intellectual vigor."

One of the most interesting studies in the Bible is the awakening intellect on the part of the men who had been touched by the Spirit. Look at Simon Peter, for example. He had been a fisherman and probably had never thought about making a speech in public in his life. But when the power of God laid hold upon him, he stood up on the day of Pentecost and spoke with an effectiveness that yielded three thousand converts. As Theodore Ferris of Boston puts it: "If anyone had said to Peter, 'I didn't know you had it in you,' he surely would have said, 'I didn't. It was the Spirit of the Lord Jesus that gave me utterance.'" The power of God, released into his life by the Spirit, touched his mind into keenness and gave to him an ability of expression the results of which cannot be denied.

On South Aycock Street in Greensboro, North Carolina, you will see a historical marker to the memory of one David Caldwell. This man was born in Pennsylvania in 1725 and for the first twenty-five years of his life had no education and worked as a carpenter and house mechanic with no further ambition. At an age when most men have completed their professional training, he had never attended grammar school. But when he was twenty-five, he attended a religious revival and was converted. Along with his spiritual awakening there came an intellectual awakening that sent him through the grades and to Princeton, where he graduated from the university and the theological school. In 1766 he went to North Carolina, settled near Greensboro, and served Buffalo and Alamance Presbyterian churches for fifty-five years. In addition he founded a school that attained the greatest reputation of all preparatory schools south of the Potomac, and brought more men into the learned professions than anyone else of his day in the South. He trained lawyers, judges, physicians, ministers, five governors of states, and had the honor himself of being offered the presidency of the University of North Carolina. Had someone who had known him in his carpenter days said to him, "I didn't know you had it in you," he would have replied, "I didn't. When the Spirit of God touched my spirit, then my mind caught fire."

That is not to say, of course, that the Holy Spirit can turn a moron into a Phi Beta Kappa, but it is to say that there are a mental energy and an insight into truth that are available for all who seek through correct means the power of God.

The expression "correct means" is put there advisedly. It has reference to a knowledge and practice of the laws that govern the operation of your mind. Let me illustrate with a personal experience.

The most difficult task a preacher faces is to be ready Sunday after Sunday with a sermon that is meaningful for his people. Yet you cannot make a sermon as you can make, say, a kite for your ten-year-old, for the materials are of a different nature. Those of you who speak and write know that you cannot command creative thought as readily as you can gather paper and sticks for a kite, and the pressure of the "relentless recurrence of the Sabbath" has driven more than one good man from the pulpit, for no preacher can sleep soundly until he has his sermon for Sunday in his mind.

For a few years my method of preparation was to select a text and get to work on it on Tuesday morning. Commentaries were consulted, and references noted in former reading were studied. Yet before beginning to write, it is essential to know where you are going, that is, to see the truth of the text organized into outline form. That is the creative part of the job, and it does not come by the clock. So in those days I used to waste one or two or three good working mornings sitting in front of the typewriter and waiting for the outline to come.

Then I remembered something I had learned some years before in a class in psychology. It was the fact that there is a part of the mind known as the subconscious that never goes to sleep. It works all the time. Like the heart and the lungs it is on a "twenty-four-hour shift." And if you know the laws that govern that part of the mind and practice them, you can save yourself much mental toil.

The first of these laws is that, if you wish the deep mind to work for you, you must first of all put your conscious mind on a definite problem and be honest enough to do your dead level best to find a solution. For my job of sermon preparation that meant I must first of all study the text in the commentaries, read the reference material, and do my best to list the points of an outline. This conscious preparation is what keeps this method of thought from becoming what one writer calls a "lazy man's free pass to heaven." The deep mind does not work for a lazy man.

Bishop Francis J. McConnell has told us how he learned that fact from sad experience. He writes:

When I was in college, I confronted one evening at eight o'clock a proposition in algebra on which I would be expected to recite the next morning. I worked as hard as I could until midnight, and then gave it up. The next morning, as I was walking down the street, admiring the beauty of the spring foliage, the solution flashed clear-cut into my mind. After I had made a perfect recitation in class, I asked myself what sense there was in all that work the night before. So I made up my mind that with the next problem I would not work till midnight, but would wait for the understanding to flash upon my mind. Something detained the flash, with disastrous consequences to my record in the class.

I was about seventeen years old, but I have never forgotten the lesson which I learned then: the sudden inspirations that amount to anything come from patient toiling which has not much of flash or suddenness about it.[1]

That experience suggests the answer that Shakespeare is reported to have made to someone who asked how he could write with such brilliance and such apparent ease: "Don't you know," he replied, "that the water which comes down as rain goes up as mist?"

That was the first law I remembered: the necessity of sustained thought by the conscious mind on the problem of an outline. The second was this: the necessity of forgetting the whole thing for a while and giving the deep mind time to do its work. When you feed lumber into a furniture factory, you do not expect to get a chair or a table the next moment. When you plant a grain of corn in the ground, you do not expect to pluck an ear of corn within the hour. It takes time to fashion the furniture and time for the seed to germinate. So when you plant your problem in the deep mind, you cannot expect it to work like a vending machine or an automat. It takes time, so the thing for you to do is to go off and forget the whole thing for a while.

Without necessarily possessing a scientific knowledge of how the mind works, you have been aware on occasions of the operation of this law. A friend asks your opinion on a subject, and you are not sure of a good answer right off the bat. You say to him, "Let me sleep on it, and then I will let you know what I think."

[1] Quoted in *In the Minister's Workshop* by Halford E. Luccock. Used by permission of Abingdon Press.

Sometime later, probably when you are least thinking about the question, an insight pops into your mind. In "sleeping on it" you were fulfilling a fundamental mental law.

I realized then that what I needed to do in harnessing this deep mind to the preparation of a sermon was to give it more time. So what I did was to move my work schedule forward one week. Instead of waiting for Tuesday before the Sunday a text was to be used, I did the reading and the thinking the Tuesday preceding. That means that in any given week I am working on two sermons: the initial reading for the sermon for Sunday week and the final writing of the sermon for the next Sunday. And in all the years that have gone by since, I cannot recall a single week when the deep mind has let me down. It has always been ready with the outline when needed.

One summer my wife and I were in London. We went to the opera, which begins there at the early hour of seven. Having had tea about four-thirty, we waited until after the performance was over for dinner. Friends had recommended Rule's Restaurant as a good place to eat, so we took a cab to that place. The building is a narrow one, wedged in between other buildings, but it has three stories with a dining room on each. Being late, we had to go to the third floor to find a table. The waiter took our order and sent it down to the kitchen on the first floor by telephone. We sat a little while and then saw the waiter answer a buzz signal. He opened a little door in the wall, and there was a dumb-waiter with our dinner all prepared and waiting to be served.

It is by some such process that the mind works. You have a problem to solve and you send your "order" downstairs to the *sub*conscious. The cooks in the kitchen there get to work, and after so long a time the dinner in the form of an answer is served up ready for use. I cannot calculate the hours of fruitless mental toil that have been saved by the operation of these laws, or the peace of mind that has come from release from a sense of pressure.

When I made this discovery for myself in 1933, I was unaware that anyone else followed such methods of work. Then a few years later I came into possession of a book by Halford E. Luccock. It was published in 1934 and is entitled *In the Minister's Workshop*. In that book Luccock has an entire chapter called "Making the Unconscious Mind an Ally." There he describes in his own inimitable way the very idea I have been presenting in this chapter, and there I learned that all creative writers, whether in the field of literature or of music, have been following this method of work from time immemorial. He quotes Robert Louis Stevenson as saying: "I used to write slow as judgment; now I write rather fast, but I am still a 'slow study' and sit a long while silent on my eggs." And Johann Strauss of his musical compositions: "At first there comes to me an idea—theme. This rests with me for months; . . . while I am busy the idea is fermenting of its own accord. Now and then I bring it distinctly to mind to see how far it has progressed."

Then Luccock quotes Graham Wallas, who has systematized these ideas in his book *The Art of Thought.* He lists the steps in order. "Preparation," which is the stage in which a problem is "investigated . . . in all directions." Then comes "Incubation," which is the waiting stage, when there is no conscious thought on the problem. And the third stage is "Illumination," when light appears and the solution comes.

I have described this process from the standpoint of a minister who is faced with the preparation of sermons, but it has its application in a much wider sense. My problem is a sermon. Yours will be something else. It may be a decision as to vocation, as to marriage, as to a business venture. I am told that business executives are now making use of this knowledge more and more commonly. They employ idea men whose task it is simply to think up new ideas. Some of them sit in a bare room with pencil and paper at a table and jot down the facts of the problem. Then they wait. I am told of one man who keeps a Bible on the table and who reads verses that can make his mind grow quiet and calm. The head of a large corporation told me once that, while he was unaware of the scientific basis of such a process, he had followed this method of solving his business problems for years.

Well, you say, what does that have to do with God? Where does he fit into the picture? The answer is, it has much to do with God, because more and more we are coming to see that the place where our minds meet the mind of God is this "deep mind" about which I have been writing.

Of course you will never find the words "deep mind" in the Bible. Its writers were not acquainted with our terminology. But you will find the word "heart" in the Bible. And when its writers use the word "heart," they mean the same thing we mean when we use the expression "deep mind." Just as the fleshly heart is the source of life in the body, so in the Bible the word "heart" is used as the seat of life or strength, that part of our beings in which exist the collective energies of the mind.

Our students of the Bible go on and tell us one more interesting fact—namely, that the deep mind is our chief point of contact with God. The Hastings Bible dictionary puts it like this: "The Bible . . . regards the 'heart' as the area of divine influence. . . . Because it is the focus of the personal life, the heart is the workplace for the appropriation and assimilation of every influence." E. Stanley Jones speaks of the subconscious as the "area of work of the Holy Spirit."

Now you are ready to understand an experience you have had like the following: You have an important decision to make and you put your mind on it and nothing happens. You forget the whole thing as best you can; and then some morning when you wake up, the answer is there as clear as daylight. You have a tendency to distrust the answer because you think it came out of your dreams, but not at all. What happened was this: Having put down all the pros and cons and received no light, you put the whole thing out of your mind. That was what you thought. What really happened was that you put it into your mind: into the part of your mind below the level of consciousness, and it is in that part of the mind that God gets to us. (It was here that God spoke to the prophets and authors of the Scripture, so that they could feel their message was not their own but was given them, and they could say, "Thus saith the Lord.") While you thought you had forgotten about the whole thing, and even during the hours of sleep, the Spirit of God was working over the raw material you provided; and then early one morning when you awakened and when this deep mind is closest to the surface, then God stepped in and handed you the solution to your problem that you were seeking.

"In all thy ways acknowledge him, and he shall direct thy paths." "In thy light shall we see light." "The Lord is my light and my salvation." That is what the Bible says, and down through the years prophet and seer and saint have put it to the test and found it true. When our Lord went into the garden to make his decision about the Cross, the way was far from clear. But when he submitted his mind to the mind of his Father—"not my will, but thine, be done"—then light came; and he walked out with a certainty that said, "Rise, men: let us be going."

In the book by Henry N. Wieman previously referred to, he speaks of this "method of solving problems" as one of the "best types of mysticism." He says:

It consists in exposing oneself to the stimulus of a problematical situation with a mind freed of all bias and preconception, and waiting in this state, or returning periodically to it, until there dawns upon the mind that integration which will solve the problem. . . . The great religious and moral and artistic insights of history have come in this way, we believe. . . . To this end we must periodically turn aside from our routine activities and wait in mystic quietude in order that more adequate insights may come to us. In this way we are able to pierce more deeply into the mystery that encompasses us, explore the unexplored, and imagine the unimagined. This is the great task of religion. It is the way man learns to live more intimately with God.[2]

Suppose now you have a problem to solve or a decision to make. What can you do to get the help of God as power for your mind to give you light upon your problem?

First of all, let go. Go back to Chapter Three and review the exercises that can relax the tension in your body and in your mind. The chances are you have been so concerned about your problem that your mind is running around in circles. It is tied in knots. You must first untangle the mental processes that are altogether unfit to do any clear thinking. I remember a college girl who came to my study. Her mind was tied in knots. She did not know what she believed, and it had "worried her sick." I suggested that, before we tackle any of the beliefs she wished to discuss we first of all get her mind in shape, and that she could come back later for the other. So on her first visit we practiced together the exercises to induce relaxation, closing with a prayer that visualized Christ. We pictured him on the stormy sea and heard him speak to the winds and the waves, "Peace, be still." We saw him work-

[2] *Op. cit.* Copyright 1929 and used by permission of The Macmillan Co.

ing the same miracle for our minds, stilling the tempest that was within us. I expected the student to return for further discussion; but a letter came a few days later, explaining that she no longer had a problem. Once she got her mental processes straightened out, all her questions seemed to answer themselves. So first of all, let go; and it will surprise you how easily mountains can become molehills.

Often, however, a second step is required. Suppose you are facing a decision concerning a marriage proposal, what vocation you will accept, or an offer of promotion with your company that calls for moving to another city. You know that no decision is right unless it is in line with the will of God. How can you get God's help in knowing what that will is?

Recall that God comes to meet us in the deep mind and that one way to get its help is first of all to put the conscious mind to work on the problem. A brilliant young man told me once that the best thing he had learned from his college training was to "think on paper." Get a sheet of paper, then draw a line down the middle from top to bottom. On one side write "For" and on the other "Against," and then list all the reasons you can think of in their proper places. In the light of them try to reach a tentative decision according to your best judgment.

Memorize these reasons; and just before you go to sleep for several nights, run over them in your mind. The deep mind is most accessible when most relaxed, and therefore just before you go to sleep is a good time to plant the seed or to feed into it the raw material upon which you wish it to work.

Then forget the whole thing for a few days and give it time to work. Of course you cannot completely put it out of your thoughts because it is such a vital matter. But at least you can make the decision that you will make no decision for the present. That will relieve the pressure and allow the process of "incubation" a chance to work. Incidentally, if you have to make speeches in public or to teach a Sunday-school class, you can save yourself much time and make a better talk if you will follow a method of preparation that allows your thoughts to "incubate." Instead of waiting until the night before you have to speak or teach to read over the lesson or form your outline, get the thing started a week in advance. You will be amazed at the manner in which everything you hear or read will turn out to be grist for your mill. The deep mind acts like a magnet which, almost unconsciously, draws to itself ideas and illustrations that fit your need.

Then you can go one step further. If you desire to give God a place in your life and wish to relate your decision to his will, picture yourself kneeling alongside Christ in the Garden. Remind yourself that God has a plan for your life, just as he had for his own Son; and that plan reaches down to your every concern. Then notice two things about his prayer.

First, he expresses a willingness to do God's will: "Not my will, but thine." Sometimes that is the hardest condition to meet, and yet it is essential. If you do not open, or yield, your eyes to a painting, you cannot see it. If you do not open, or yield, your mind to a thought, you cannot understand it. If you do not open, or yield, your will to God's will, you cannot know it. So you kneel with your Master in the Garden and you pray his prayer after him: "Thy will be done." And you can be sure that God always meets a man on the spot of self-surrender.

Finally, Jesus kept on praying. It is recorded that three times he repeated his prayer. What you can learn from that fact is this: If you expect light to come, then it is only common sense to keep looking in the direction from which you expect it to shine. In one of his lessons on prayer our Lord said this: "Ask, and it shall be given you; seek, and ye shall find; knock, and it shall be opened unto you." The tense of these verbs in the Greek is the imperfect, indicating a continuous action. So what Jesus is saying is this: Ask, and keep on asking; seek, and keep on seeking; knock, and keep on knocking.

And when the door opens for you, you will find yourself ushered into the blessed peace of his holy will.

CHAPTER SIX

POWER TO LIVE AT YOUR BEST

In this chapter we continue our study of the power of God for daily living. We remember what James Stewart and Alexis Carrel said about prayer as being the source of power on physical, mental, moral, and spiritual levels. Having considered the first two of these, we turn now to the third.

"I have had more trouble with myself than with any other man I ever met." This statement by D. L. Moody has often been quoted, because it is so true to life. Most of us do have a lot of trouble with ourselves, due to our dual nature of dust and deity. There is one part of us that honestly intends to be clean and kind and honest and forgiving; and there is another part of us that makes us have thoughts we ought not to have and indulge in dreams for which we are ashamed and say things about people we are later sorry for. The classic statement of that fact comes from Paul, who wrote, "The good that I would I do not: but the evil which I would not, that I do." It would seem that we have here a good man and another not so good living in the same person, and the problem this fact poses is how to change the one who is not so desirable into the nature of the other.

The same writer who states the problem so well for

us provides later on in the same letter the clue to its solution. He says, "Be ye transformed by the renewing of your mind." He seems to indicate that the mind is the key to the man and that the way to become a transformed person is the refashioning of the mind. Moffatt takes this statement and makes that fact as clear as daylight. "Have your mind renewed," he says, "and so be transformed in nature." Let us see how we can begin right there and put this truth to work.

The first thing to note is that your mind is a much more complex affair than you would normally suppose. Here and there in the preceding pages I have spoken of the subconscious or deep mind, but I have not had much to say about its real nature. Scholars are pretty well agreed as to its reality—namely, that below the level of consciousness there exists more of what we call mind. It will come as welcome news to some of us that we have more mind than that of which we are conscious!

It does not take much reflection to understand how that can be true. For example, a part of your thinking process is occupied with the area of immediate awareness. In the focus of your attention are certain facts of which you are immediately aware. At the present time you are conscious of sitting in your room in your chair, with perhaps a member or two of your family with you, while you read this book. But you know also that there is another area of your mind that is occupied by thoughts that are not in the focus of attention, but that can be recalled at any moment you wish. If the book loses interest for you, you can immediately retreat from the present into the past and begin to think of the good time you had last summer at the beach or yesterday at the football or baseball game. The beach and the game while in the past are still in your mind. So when you see the fact of these two areas, that of immediate awareness and that which can be recalled at will, it is not difficult to go on and believe what the experts tell us, that there is still another area of which we are entirely unconscious.

The picture that is used to describe this area of the mind is that of the *iceberg*. I have never seen an iceberg, but we are told that seven eighths of the bulk of an iceberg is below the level of water. So it is with your mind. Only a fraction of it is above the level of your consciousness; by far the larger part of it is buried down there below the surface in what is called the subconscious.

Another word that is used to describe this part of your mind is the word *factory*. Your deep mind is always at work, even while you are asleep. It takes the thoughts that you feed into it during your waking hours as raw material, and it works on them all the time. You have boasted, have you not, that you do not need an alarm clock to wake you up at a certain time. If you wish to get up at six-thirty, you merely set the clock of your mind—and sure enough, you wake up. It is your deep mind that does it for you.

This truth has turned the light on a certain verse in the Bible for me. Long ago I read this sentence: "He giveth his beloved sleep." That did not mean anything to me, but when I learned that scholars say the verse really means "He giveth his beloved *in* sleep," that began to make sense. You have discovered, I am sure, that if you go to sleep with thoughts of anxiety and fear in your mind, you will be doubly fearful and anxious when you awaken; but if you go to sleep with thoughts of confidence and peace and the power of God to meet your needs you will awaken with a deepened sense of adequacy and ability to meet your duties. It is interesting to notice that the wisdom of the race led our parents to teach us to say our prayers just before we go to sleep at night and just after we get up in the morning. In other words, we were taught to make ourselves conscious of God's presence precisely at those two points in the day when we are most relaxed and when, therefore, the deep mind is most accessible. "He giveth his beloved *in* sleep."

There is another verse in the Bible that meant absolutely nothing to me until I saw it in the light of the deep mind. Our Lord said once, "Every idle word that men shall speak, they shall give account thereof in the day of judgment." That has no meaning until you learn that everything you say or think or do, your slips of tongue and acts of absent-mindedness, are symptoms of your unconscious thoughts. You never in your life, for example, forgot a date with your girl friend, but more than once you have forgotten a date with your dentist. You honestly did not intend to forget it, but your deep mind told you it would be painful and so protected you by making you forget it. That is the reason your little boy forgets to come home and mow the lawn, and why your opponent has a way of forgetting how many strokes he played on the last hole in golf. To paraphrase a famous line: "The mind has reasons the mind knows not of." As your guest is leaving, you intend to say, "I wish you would stay longer," but your face turns red when what you actually say is this: "I wish you wouldn't stay so long." And so you see now what Jesus means by the "idle word." As T. R. Glover puts it: "The idle word is to condemn a man, not because it is idle but because, being unstudied, it speaks of his heart and reveals, unconsciously but plainly, what he *is* in reality."

So then we begin the attack on our problem by noting that your mind is a complex affair by reason of the fact of its depth in the subconscious.

Move on now and notice a second fact: Your life is controlled more by that deep mind than by your surface mind. David Seabury claims that "all of our real thinking, and three-quarters of our mental activity, transpires below the level of our awareness, and only comes to the surface as the time of active use arrives." Charles Mayo corroborates that claim by declaring before a medical association in Chicago that 75 per cent of human action is controlled by the unconscious and only 25 per cent by conscious thought.

For example, a doctor named Bernard Hart gives us the following story:

One of my patients, a former Sunday school teacher, had become a convinced atheist. He insisted that he had reached that standpoint after long and careful study of the literature on the subject and, as a matter of fact, he really had ac-

LETTING GOD HELP YOU

quired a remarkably wide knowledge of religious apologetics. He discoursed at length upon the evidence, marshalling his arguments with considerable skill and producing a coherent and well-reasoned case. Subsequent psychological analysis, however, revealed the real complex responsible for his atheism: the girl to whom he had been engaged had eloped with the most enthusiastic of his fellow Sunday school teachers. We see that in this patient the causal complex, resentment against his successful rival, had expressed itself by a repudiation of the beliefs which had formerly constituted the principal bond between them. The arguments, the study, the quotations, were merely an elaborate rationalization.[1]

So it is that many of the things you do, entirely unknown to yourself, are governed by this deep mind down below the level of consciousness.

And now we come upon another fact concerning this deep mind that adds difficulty to our problem: It is by nature evil. It is in that part of your mind below the level of consciousness that you get human nature in the raw. It is there that the instincts, like sex and the ego, reign supreme. It is from those depths that your dreams arise, and it is out of that abyss that your impure thoughts are born. Jesus did not use the language of modern science, but a modern scientist named Kunkel pays him this compliment: "The existence of our unconscious desires and our repressed tendencies could not be described more strikingly" than in these words: "You are like tombs whitewashed; they look comely on the outside, but inside they are full of dead

[1] Quoted in *Souls in the Making* by John G. McKenzie. Copyright 1929 and used by permission of The Macmillan Co.

80

men's bones and all manner of impurity." It must be because it is so true that for many years I have remembered word for word a statement I read from a Frenchman named La Rochefoucauld: "I have never examined the heart of a wicked man," he says; "I once became acquainted with the heart of a good man: I was shocked."

For example, Charles T. Holman tells this story:

In the town where I was born lived a woman and her daughter, who walked in their sleep. One night while silence enfolded the world, the woman and her daughter, walking yet asleep, met in the mist-veiled garden. And the mother spoke and she said: "At last, at last, my enemy! You by whom my life was destroyed—who built up your life upon the ruins of mine! Would I could kill you!" And the daughter spoke and she said: "O hateful woman, selfish and old! Who stand between my free self and men! Who would have my life an echo of your faded life! Would you were dead!" At that moment the cock crew, and both women awoke. The mother said gently, "Is that you, darling?" And the daughter answered gently, "Yes, dear!" [2]

And *there* you have the reason why so often we find the good life a difficult achievement. The conscious mind is civilized, but the deep mind is savage. The conscious mind is Christian, but the deep mind is pagan. The conscious mind has been converted, but the deep mind is still unregenerate. And as a result you have a major conflict going on within yourself. Even after your conscious mind has accepted the Chris-

[2] Quoted in *How to Be a Transformed Person* by E. Stanley Jones. Used by permission of Abingdon Press.

tian way, you are sitting on top of a volcano. You are like a ship whose starboard turbines are pushing forward with its port engines backing up. One part of you says, "Get thee behind me, Satan," and another part says, "Get back there and push me on." Now you see what the Apostle means when he says, "I find then a law, that, when I would do good, evil is present with me." And so he says: "For I delight in the law of God after the inward man: But I see another law in my members, warring against the law of my mind, and bringing me into captivity to the law of sin which is in my members."

And so we come now to the point of the matter: the conversion of the deep mind. That means that in order really to become a transformed person you require two conversions. There is first the conversion of the conscious mind, and that happens when you commit yourself to Christ and decide you are going to play on his team. But more than that, you will never get rid of inner conflict and find any pleasure in the Christian life until you go on to that second conversion, the conversion of the deep mind. And this, I believe, is what the apostle means when he says in Romans: "Have your mind renewed, and so be transformed in nature." How then can that be done?

The answer to that question lies in a law of human nature that says we become like what we live with. You may have heard about the little boy who used a bad word one Christmas day and when his mother asked him where in the world he had heard such a word used, answered, "That's what Santa Claus said when he

stubbed his toe on a chair in my room last night."
When Bobby Jones was a little boy, his family lived
near the East Lake golf course in Atlanta, and every
afternoon after school he followed the club pro around
the course, watching him play. When he grew up and
began to play himself, his golf swing was a perfect
imitation of that of the pro. It is a law of life that we
become like what we live with.

The same law holds when you turn from the out-
ward to the inner life. A friend telephoned me one day
to say that she has always done a lot of public speaking
without any trouble, but that lately she had begun to
suffer from stage fright and asked if there was anything she could do about it. Banking on this law, I
suggested that, when she had a speech coming up, she
practice a certain method. Every night for a week just
before she dropped off to sleep, I suggested that she
picture herself standing before the audience and see
herself in her mind's eye delivering her speech easily
and well and with perfect composure. She told me
later on that the method worked. It was bound to work,
because it is a law. If you live with an image of yourself as being a certain kind of person, you will in time
become that kind of person.

Another person went to see his minister and said that
temper was his problem. He was always losing his
temper, and it was just about ruining his home life.
What could he do about it? His minister suggested
that every morning at breakfast he get his wife to read
with him those words from I Corinthians that describe
love as being very patient, and then that every night,

before he went to sleep, he picture himself in the presence of Christ and see himself controlling his temper and showing real patience in the midst of a situation that had been getting his goat. The man came back later to tell his minister that this worked. It had to work, because it is a law. We become like what we live with, whether outwardly or inwardly. If we live with a picture of ourselves as always losing our temper, we will keep on losing our temper; whereas if we live with a picture of ourselves in the presence of Christ, we will begin to have the kind of love that is patient. The apostle states that law in a different way in another place. He says: Beholding as a mirror the character of our Lord, little by little we are changed into the same likeness.

Now put that same truth in terms of modern science; and what it says is this: You can remake the subconscious, and then the subconscious will remake you. If you will take the trouble to form those pictures of yourself as the kind of person you wish to become, persistently enough, then you can renew your deep mind; and then your deep mind, which controls 75 per cent of your actions, will transform your nature.

There is another verse in the Bible you will never understand until you see that fact. Our Lord said once:

The good man brings good out of his good store,
and the evil man brings evil out of his store of evil.
(Moffatt.)

He thus pictures this deep mind as a bank. You can't draw out of a bank something you have not first put

84

in. And every time you make a deposit of a good thought, a good deed, a good attitude, you build up your balance in the "good store"; and this "good store" in the factory that is the deep mind works even while you are asleep and begins to transform your nature. Thus the deep mind that left to itself is a terrific drag on the good life can actually be made to work in your favor. "The good man brings good out of his good store."

Long years ago I read a story about an old Negro man who lived in Asheville, North Carolina. His name was Uncle Barney, and he had the kind of religion that was attractive. He seemed to have a good time being good, and everybody who knew him liked him and wanted some of his kind of religion. Then one day he told his secret.

He happened to be a local Methodist preacher, and the presiding elder was in town. He called his preachers together and told them he was going to have an old-fashioned experience meeting. He wanted them to tell how they conducted family worship at home. One by one they went round the circle. When Uncle Barney's turn came, he rose and said he couldn't have family worship at his house because he was a bachelor. "But," he said, "every morning when I get up and wash my face, I say, 'O Lord Jesus, wash me clean from sin today.' And when I put on my clothes, I say, 'O Lord Jesus, clothe me in the garments of righteousness this day.' And when I put on my shoes, I say, 'O Lord Jesus, get in these shoes with me and make me walk in your steps this day.' " And after that everybody

knew why Uncle Barney had a religion that was so con-
tagiously attractive. Out of his good store that good
man brought forth good. He had his mind renewed in
his daily rendezvous with the Master, so he was transformed in his nature.

There was an old French saint who used to go into
the cathedral in Ars and sit for long periods of time.
One day someone asked him what he and the Lord did
all that time he was sitting in the cathedral. His answer
was, "I just look at him, and he just looks at me."

James Stewart has this to say about the change that
transformed the men in the New Testament:

Look at those men again. Many of them had spent half
a lifetime at the beck and call of devouring, devastating pas-
sions; many of them had had wasted, shrivelled, burnt-out
souls—until Jesus had got hold of them, and by a miracle
of grace had wrenched them clear and set them with their
faces to the sky; and now there they were, walking through
cities that were living dens of corruption, and yet clad in
the purity of Christ! Ask any one of them how it happened.
"It is not I," comes the answer, "but the Spirit of God in
me." [3]

That is a power all of us need; and the question is,
How can you get it? How can Jesus get hold of you so
that, when you leave home in the morning, or on the
week end, or for a trip to a convention, you will know
that when you get back home you will be as clean as
when you left?

The answer lies in your interior companionships.

[3] *Op. cit.* Used by permission of Chas. Scribner's Sons and T. & T.
Clark.

You know there are some persons in whose presence you are always at your best, while there are others who seem always to pull you down to less than your best. At the top of the list of the former is one whose name is Jesus. When you think of him as being beside you, it is easier to change and be your best than not to change. I dare you to look Christ in the eye and then do the dishonorable thing, if you can!

Some years ago there lived in London a man named Quentin Hogg, whose hobby was to reclaim the lives of the boys who lived in the streets. One of these boys was named Jem Nicholls, and one day Hogg was talking to Jem and asked him how the fight for character was coming on. "It's pretty much of an uphill battle," Jem replied; "but you know I carry a picture of you in my pocket, and whenever I am tempted, I take it out and look at it and it helps. You know, Mr. Hogg, I believe if I could always be with you, I would never have any trouble whipping the devil." And his friend said, "Well, Jem, I can't be with you all the time, but I can tell you about Somebody who will." And then he took out his New Testament and read the words of our Lord: I will never go away; I will be with you every day.

Creative silence is never more creative than when spent as the saint in the cathedral at Ars spent it. "They that wait upon the Lord shall renew their strength." There is no better way in the world of waiting upon the Lord than of carrying the picture of Christ in your mind. You can take it out and look at it before you leave home in the morning, you can live with it all through the day, and you can achieve that same moral grandeur that belonged to the apostle, for you can say with him: "I live; yet not I, but Christ liveth in me."

Years ago I learned the following lines, and their beauty lingers still:

> A Persian fable says, One day
> A wanderer found a lump of clay,
> So redolent of sweet perfume
> Its odors scented all the room.
> "What art thou?" was his quick demand;
> "Art thou some gem from Samarcand,
> Or spikenard in rude disguise,
> Or other costly merchandise?"
> "Nay, I am but a lump of clay."
> "Then, whence this wondrous perfume, say?"
> "Friend, if the secret I disclose,
> I have been dwelling with the rose."
> Sweet parable! And will not those
> Who dwell with Sharon's Rose
> Distill sweet odors all around
> Though low and mean themselves are found?
> Dear Lord, abide with us, that we
> May draw our perfume fresh from Thee.

CHAPTER SEVEN

POWER FROM
AN UNSEEN PRESENCE

You will remember the famous trial of the Communists in New York when Judge Harold R. Medina was on the bench. The defendants resorted to tactics designed to break the health of the judge and force him from the bench, and for a while the whole country was apprehensive lest they succeed.

Judge Medina is a vestryman in the Episcopal Church in Westhampton, New York, and in an address before the annual dinner of the Church Club of New York he told how he was kept from breaking down:

It took me a long time to realize what the Communists were trying to do to me—to wear me down until I lost my self-control and occasioned a mistrial. But as I felt myself getting weaker and weaker, and found the burden more and more difficult to bear, I sought strength where I have sought it all my life, from the one Source that never fails.

One day, doubtless due to previous planning, a defendant refused to answer a question. He pleaded a supposed Constitutional privilege which obviously had no application. I gave him time to consult with his counsel about it. I held the matter in abeyance overnight to make sure that I was making no misapplication of the law. And I prayed.

The next day . . . I sentenced that defendant to prison for 30 days, unless he should sooner purge himself of contempt by answering the question.

As I finished pronouncing sentence, pandemonium broke loose in the courtroom. The other ten defendants and their lawyers, and many of the spectators, rose to their feet; there was a great shouting and hullabaloo, and in the midst of the din several of the defendants charged toward the bench. Yet, in all the excitement, I felt perfectly calm. I did not raise my voice over my usual tones, as I singled out several of those men, identified the language they were using, got it on the record, and sentenced each of them also to imprisonment for the remainder of the trial.

I want to make it clear that my unguided will alone, and self-control as I possess, would have been unequal to this test. If ever a man felt the presence of Someone else beside him, strengthening his will and giving him aid and comfort, it was I on that day.

And so it was again, toward the end of August, when the uproar and confusion of the Communists was so distracting that I finally had to leave the courtroom and lie down in my chambers. Let me be frank: I was thinking then that perhaps I should never go back. In my weakness it seemed to me at last that I had stood as much as I could for as long as I could. I could not endure more of it. I was ready to give up.

But, instead, like a frightened child calling to his father in the dark, I asked God to take charge of things and that His will be done. I cannot report any mysterious or supernatural experience as a result of that prayer. All I know is that, as I lay on the couch in the heat of that darkened chamber, some kind of new strength seemed to flow into my veins. That brief period of communion with my Maker saved my life and saved the trial. After 15 minutes I was refreshed, and went back to carry on the business of my court.

And I gained in strength from that moment on to the end.[1]

Someone has defined courage as the ability to hold on one minute longer. Spiritual strength is the power of the spirit to hold on one minute longer in faith, in patience, in courage, in endurance. There are persons who give you the impression of great energy; they can do a great deal, but when you come down to it, they cannot endure much. There are other persons who give you the impression of deep resources of interior power. No matter what the strain, they stand like a rock. This power is important too, because it is plain that what we can do depends in some cases upon how much we can stand without going to pieces. This power seems to come from down deep inside, from your spirit; and the secret is that your spirit is in touch with the Spirit that is God. What we are concerned with chiefly in these pages is how we can make contact with the Source and find strength in order to become happy, healthy, wholesome persons.

Take, for example, the common experience of fear. It has been called Private Enemy Number One, and the toll it takes is tremendous. A famous psychologist says that fear is the "most disintegrating enemy of human personality." The old Anglo-Saxon word for worry carries a picture of a wolf catching a sheep by the throat. It is a picture of destruction, and that is exactly what fear does. It destroys. It destroys the health of our bodies, and the peace of our mind, and the

[1] From "Someone Else on the Bench," *The Reader's Digest,* August, 1951. Used by permission of *The Reader's Digest* and Judge Harold R. Medina.

efficiency of our acts. A minister friend told me he was performing a marriage ceremony for a couple and the groom seemed to be scared out of his wits. The minister said, "Say after me: I, John, take thee, Mary, to be my wedded wife, . . . for better, for worse, for richer, for poorer," and so on. The groom got his tongue twisted, and what he said was this: "I, John, take thee, Mary, to be my wedded wife, . . . from better to worse, from richer to poorer. . . ." He was filled with fear, and fear had robbed him of his normal powers of speech. It is guilty of far more serious burglaries, and the conquest of fear is one of our foremost needs.

It is easy for a minister to say to his counselee: "The cure for fear is faith. Jesus said, 'Fear not.' As a Christian you ought to obey his command and exercise the faith that can conquer fear." There are plenty of people who have faith yet who still have also their fears. What we need is a knowledge of *how* we can make our faith work so as to cure our fears. It seems to me that the method outlined in these pages for laying hold upon the power of God is admirably suited to the cure of fear in two ways.

For one thing, the letting go in physical relaxation, which has been suggested as a preparation for prayer, is a perfect first step in getting rid of fear. You see that fact at work in the old story of the Negro mammy who was asked why it was she never worried, and she said: "When I works, I works hard; when I sits, I sits loose; and when I worries, I goes to sleep." She may not have known it of course, but she had medical science on her side. Whatever it was that she did to learn to sit loose, to release the tension that ties us in knots, that was what relaxed her body and cured her worry.

For example, David Fink has analyzed fear in five steps. He says that the first is a sense of danger and the second is a desire to escape. If a little boy sees a big dog in the yard, he has first a sense of danger and tries to run away. But if the gate is shut and he cannot escape, then his insides begin running away. That is the sensation of tenseness you feel when you say you are tied in knots inside; and that is the third step in the process of the development of fear, which the doctor describes as "bodily responses that follow the intellectual factors of a sense of danger and a desire to escape." The fourth step is a disagreeable sensation caused by these bodily responses that leads to number five—namely, a secondary motive to find relief in safety. Then if safety is impossible, these feelings become so intense as to produce paralyzing terror.

Then Fink points out this important fact: "You end your fear when you stop the process in any one of these five activities." For example, you are afraid of burglars when you hear unusual noises in the living room. Shaking from head to foot, you tiptoe to the door and peep in. It's just a window shade blowing in the wind. You killed your fear in its first stage: the sense of danger.

Or, he says, you are afraid of climbing a mountain. The very thought of the narrow footpath on the edge of the canyon makes you shiver. But after you practice it a few times, you no longer desire to escape from the situation. You learn to enjoy the thrill of danger, so you kill fear in the second stage.

Or you are afraid of some duty that lies ahead of you. The very thought of having to make a speech in public, of interviewing an important prospect, of taking care of your first baby after the nurse leaves and you are on your own—any one of a number of situations gives you a sense of danger, and you desire to escape. But you must make that speech; you must see that prospect; you must take care of your child. When you realize you cannot escape, then you get that tight feeling in the pit of your stomach. Your mind begins to talk to your body, and you feel all tense. If, however, you will force your mind to talk to your body in other terms, in terms of quietness and confidence and tranquillity and serenity, then you will kill your fear in its third stage. It is impossible to be both relaxed and tense at the same time; and it is the tautness, the being "frozen stiff," that leads on to the fourth and fifth steps, which constitute the harmful results. When you relax the body, you sidetrack the fear that started in the mind.

So it is that you can write down in one-two-three fashion the reason why letting go will help cure your worries and your fears and your anxieties. There is, however, a second way by which our faith can fit into this need.

When the movie "Snow White and the Seven Dwarfs" was first advertised on the billboards, the mothers in our city promised to take their young children. It was discovered, however, that there was a terrifying picture of a witch on the screen, and these mothers were concerned lest such a horror scene might set up unhealthy fears. But a promise is a promise with a child, so they worked out this solution to their dilemma. They took the children to the movie, all right; but just before the witch came on, they got up and went out. During that week the small son of friends of ours was playing one afternoon with some older boys. He said he was going to see "Snow White" that night. From the vantage point of their seniority the older boys said, "You'll have to leave when the witch comes on."

"No, I'm not," he said.

"Yes, you will."

"No, I'll not."

"Well, why won't you then?"

"Because," he replied, "I'm going with my daddy; and when the old witch comes on, I'm not going to look at the witch. I'm just going to look at my daddy."

You just cannot find any better expression of real religion than that! That is faith at work, sure enough. "When the old witch comes on, I'm not going to look at the witch. I'm just going to look at my daddy." Not only do we let go, but we let God. We put him in the center of our attention in our prayer and affirm his presence and then: "Thou will keep him in perfect peace, whose mind is stayed on thee." "In quietness and confidence shall be your strength." "It is I, have no fear." (Moffatt.)

I have found in these two steps of the pathway to power a most satisfactory method of helping people

95

to find in their faith the "invisible means of support" that they need. My study is equipped with a lounging chair, the back of which reclines; and it provides the ideal posture for physical relaxation as described by David Fink. After my visitor explains his need, we practice together the exercises suggested in Chapter Three. Having released the tension in body and mind and unblocked the channel, then one is ready to receive the strength of God. I select from the Bible verses that affirm the answer to a particular need. If the problem is one of inner inadequacy, then the theme of scriptural truth would be, "My grace is sufficient for thee." If it is a lack of serenity, then: "In quietness and confidence shall be your strength." If it is weakness in the face of temptation, then: "[He] will not suffer you to be tempted above that ye are able; but will with the temptation also make a way to escape." If it is trouble in a marriage because of temper, then Paul's words about love as being patient and kind provide a mirror and a pattern. In this way faith is more than faith: it is God supplying our every "need according to his riches in glory by Christ Jesus." And prayer is more than prayer: it is a means of "plugging in on the power of the universe." It is being "strengthened with might by [God's] spirit in the inner man."

I have been interested to discover that the above method of dealing with spiritual needs is in substantial agreement with a technique described by John A. Schindler, chairman of the Department of Medicine of the Monroe Clinic in Wisconsin, in dealing with persons whose illness is emotionally induced. In his book titled *How to Live 365 Days a Year* he speaks of his own method as based on a concept that is the

direct antithesis of Freudian psychiatry, which has been oriented by the concept that emotional stress is conditioned early in life by an unacceptable experience that is relegated to the dusky murkiness of the subconscious, where it preys on the host forevermore. . . . Being interested mainly in the past, the traditional psychiatrist often prefers to do very little about the present or the future. . . . [But] emotional stress can be helped *only by learning* to react to situations RIGHT NOW with equanimity, courage, determination, and cheerfulness. The person who learns to handle the majority of life situations with equanimity, courage, determination, and cheerfulness has taken a long step into maturity. . . . My method of therapy places the patient on the enjoyment principle by a conditioned reflex through conscious thought control, by substituting equanimity, courage, determination, and cheerfulness, whenever anxiety, apprehension, and so on, begin to make their appearances. This substitution is done by conscious thought control until habit can eventually take over.[2]

In other words, Schindler believes that most can be done for his patient by re-educating his mind toward emotional maturity through conscious thought control. The pathway to power utilizes the same technique. It diagnoses the need, selects the particular truth of God that speaks to that need, and through conscious thought control, which is another name for prayer, it remakes

[2] Reprinted by permission from *How to Live 365 Days a Year*, by John A. Schindler, M.D., pp. 206-208. Copyright, 1954, by Prentice-Hall, Inc., Englewood Cliffs, N.J.

the mind and so the life. And yet it has this additional advantage: It is based upon the conviction that God's will is our good, and his power is behind his will.

At the risk of being misunderstood, let me quote part of a letter. It came from a woman who had visited my study as a total stranger three years before she wrote the letter. That was my only meeting with her, and she wrote from a distant state. My reason for quoting the letter is the hope that it might make these pages more credible and encourage you to begin such a practice of the presence of God for yourself.

Dear Dr. Redhead:

In the fall of 1953, I came to you with a problem bigger than I could solve—and apparently I was trying to solve it on my own. I knew that Help existed, as I had been subjected to religious training from cradle roll on up; but somewhere along the line I missed the "How" of that "Help." At the time I really needed results; and I failed to get strength because the fault was in me, not in what I was seeking. . . .

I went home from your office that day; and about as much as I could say to my sister was that I had heard many prayers and had offered many prayers—but somehow that day it was different. At the time I had allowed so much tension to build up in my nerves that it had caused a short circuit and had blocked the channel from which power can come. Consequently I couldn't take in too much of the meaning of your prayer—but the channel was unblocked enough to know there was a Presence with us.

After returning to my home, I spent many hours alone in an effort to "get through"; and I did receive strength, and strength in abundance. . . . From the minute I started practicing what you had passed on to me through our Lord, I felt myself growing in a spiritual way.

I have noticed that whenever anyone catches the the idea and understands the reasons for the various steps involved and then puts them into practice, he gets results.

During the early days of World War II in the Pacific, an American soldier who had been through the campaign on Guadalcanal came home on furlough. The unorthodox methods of warfare with snipers firing from behind every tree had made our men jittery and had just about ruined the morale of our troops. The Defense Department called this soldier to Washington and asked if he had any suggestions as to how soldiers could be better prepared to face the nerve-shattering experience of jungle warfare. His answer brought the whole department to attention, for what he said was this: "Teach them the twenty-third psalm."

How can you learn the twenty-third psalm so that you can say and mean it, "The Lord is my shepherd; I shall not want"? How can you find the spiritual strength you need to restore your soul?

Once again the answer lies in the pathway to power. First of all, learn to let go. Practice the exercises that can release the tensions within you and bring relaxation. The deep mind is most accessible when you are most relaxed. When you have unblocked the channel, you are ready to receive the strength that God gives. Remember to "visualize" and then to "verbalize." Picture yourself as being in the presence of Christ and listen to him as he talks.

I have found that many people do not know enough Bible verses to continue the practice of the presence of God for a length of time sufficient to bring results. For that reason I am closing this chapter with an "Alphabet of Affirmations" that I use constantly. All you have to do is to associate one word in the verse with each letter of the alphabet; and before you know it, you have twenty-six verses at your command.

As you read your Bible, you will find other verses that say the thing you need to have said and that become a veritable Word of God to your spirit. As these accumulate, you will find yourself building other alphabets, suited to particular areas of need.

AN ALPHABET OF AFFIRMATIONS

A—Acquaint now thyself with him, and be at peace: thereby good shall come unto thee. (Job 22:21.)

B—Be still, and know that I am God. (Ps. 46:10.)

C—Come unto me, all ye that labour and are heavy laden, and I will give you rest. (Matt. 11:28.)

D—Draw nigh to God, and he will draw nigh to you. (Jas. 4:8.)

E—Every one that asketh receiveth; and he that seeketh findeth; and to him that knocketh it shall be opened. (Matt. 7:8.)

F—Fear not, for I am with thee. (Gen. 26:24.)

G—God is our refuge and strength, a very present help in trouble. (Ps. 46:1.)

H—Happy is he that hath the God of Jacob for his help. (Ps. 146:5.)

I—I will both lay me down in peace, and sleep: for thou, Lord, only makest me dwell in safety. (Ps. 4:8.)

J—Joy cometh in the morning. (Ps. 30:5.)

K—Know ye that the Lord he is God. (Ps. 100:3.)

L—Lo, I am with you alway. (Matt. 28:20.)

M—My God shall supply all your need. (Phil. 4:19.)

N—Nevertheless I am continually with thee. (Ps. 73:23.)

O—O Lord of hosts, blessed is the man that trusteth in thee. (Ps. 84:12.)

P—Peace I leave with you, my peace I give unto you. (John 14:27.)

Q—In quietness and in confidence shall be your strength. (Isa. 30:15.)

R—The Lord is my shepherd. . . . He restoreth my soul. (Ps. 23:1, 3.)

S—Surely goodness and mercy shall follow me all the days of my life. (Ps. 23:6.)

T—Thou wilt keep him in perfect peace, whose mind is stayed on thee. (Isa. 26:3.)

U—Underneath are the everlasting arms. (Deut. 33:27.)

V—Verily I say unto you, If ye have faith as a grain of mustard seed, . . . nothing shall be impossible unto you. (Matt. 17:20.)

W—Wait on the Lord: be of good courage, and he shall strengthen thine heart: wait, I say, on the Lord. (Ps. 27:14.)

X—[He] is able to do exceeding abundantly above all that we ask or think. (Eph. 3:20.)

Y—Yea, though I walk through the valley of the shadow of death, I will fear no evil: for thou art with me. (Ps. 23:4.)

Z—Let the children of Zion be joyful in their King. (Ps. 149:2.)

CHAPTER EIGHT

LAGNIAPPE

In the last four chapters we have had a look at the forms in which power for living can be known in experience. We can know it on the levels of the physical, mental, moral, and spiritual. After having traveled the pathway to power in its two steps of letting go and letting God, I discovered there were certain extra benefits that it bestows for the religious life.

As a boy in Louisiana I became acquainted with a Creole word called "lagniappe." When Mother sent me to the grocery store to make a purchase, the grocer wrapped up the package and I paid him, and then he usually gave me a piece or two of candy. That was something extra, something over and above. I have found that the pathway to power has its own lagniappe. The book of Job has a word for it: "Acquaint now thyself with him [with God], and be at peace: thereby good shall come unto thee." What are some of the good things that come to us once we know God in the manner that has been described?

The first one Job mentions by name; it is something that he calls "peace." That interests us because peace of mind is an expression about which we hear much today. Let a minister speak of peace of mind and he will discover how much in demand it is. Let an author write a book on peace of mind and it will sell like hot cakes.

Now there are two ways in which you can think about this business of peace of mind. The first is to make it an end in itself and to seek it for its sake alone. This, I think, is the basis for the criticism of the so-called peace of mind cult in contemporary religious life. Our time has been called the age of anxiety, and there is certainly a deep inner restlessness in people. So the preacher finds an expression like "peace of mind," and he promises its possession. Then the critic steps up and says that the child of God has no right to any peace as long as so many things are wrong in our world, and the desire for it is wrong because it is nothing but a desire to escape from the unpleasant task of setting right these wrongs. And of course any intelligent person sees a lot of sense in that criticism.

But there is another way of thinking about this business of peace of mind, and it is related to the question of power. Harry Emerson Fosdick gave the best definition of peace I ever heard over the radio many years ago, and it has never left my mind. Peace, he said, is power in reserve, greater than you need. For example, peace in business is the consciousness of capital in plenty. Peace in daily life is the consciousness of health and ability to spare. Peace on an automobile trip is the knowledge of a full tank of gasoline and a spare tire in the trunk. Peace in the home is the consciousness of love over and above the petty disturbances of family living. Peace in the soul is the consciousness of the presence of an unseen friend and that over and around and beneath life there are available the resources that will prove more than enough for our needs. Peace of mind is a margin of power in reserve, greater than your needs. So it is that the pathway to power is likewise the path to peace.

Our Lord certainly did not seek peace as an end in itself. He never once sought to escape the hard realities of his mission. He "stedfastly set his face to go to Jerusalem," knowing full well all that it would mean. Yet you cannot deny that there was a deep sense of peace at the core of his being. "Ye . . . shall leave me alone," he said to his closest friends: "and yet I am not alone, because the Father is with me." In that fellowship with the Father he found a source of power over and above his needs, and from that power he gained peace. "Peace I leave with you, my peace I give unto you: not as the world giveth, give I unto you. [What that means is this: The world cannot give it to you, neither can the world take it away from you, because it comes from God.] Let not your heart be troubled, neither let it be afraid."

When someone asked a college student why he liked a certain chapel speaker, he said this: "Because when that man speaks, he gives me the feeling that I hold in my hand an ace that can trump any trick life deals to me." That is the feeling you have when once you know the power of God through prayer. It is the peace that comes from a margin of power in reserve, greater than your need. In that sense Job is correct: "Acquaint now thyself with him, and be at peace."

Then the ancient writer goes on to add this phrase:

"thereby good shall come unto thee." A further good thing that will come to you once you know prayer as power is a new enthusiasm for the practice of the presence of God in prayer and the reading of the Bible.

You know of course that as a professing Christian you ought to read the Bible, but the simple truth is that you do not. I suppose there is no other best seller that is so little read as this book. Why? Well, you started out some years ago in high enthusiasm. You began where you would begin reading any book, at the beginning. But before you got very far, you found yourself stuck in the middle of Leviticus, and you have never become unstuck. Your conscience hurts you because you do not read it any more, yet you have never found enough good in the habit to begin again.

The same is true about prayer. You know that as a Christian you ought to pray. You promised when you joined the church to keep your friendship with God in constant repair. You meant what you said, and you started out in high enthusiasm. But before many years you gave it up. Why? Because you did not have the sense of anybody being there. You felt that your prayers did not reach any higher than your head, as you put it, and that you could not "get through." You thought of your prayer as a kind of pious soliloquy, a spiritual gymnastic, nothing but dumbbell exercise. And because there was no lift in the experience, it became a burden too heavy to be borne, so you have tossed it overboard. Of course your conscience hurts you about it, but it hasn't hurt enough to lead you back into the practice of prayer as a daily habit. The only times you

105

have prayed in recent years have been the times when you had a problem too big for you, and you called on God as a kind of last resort.

Now prayer as a pathway to power will change all that. I remember one day feeling far spent, altogether inadequate for the demands of my work, and then sitting down to read Paul's letter to his friends in Philippi. All of a sudden I came upon this statement: "My God shall supply all your need." These words turned on a stop light, and I could read no further. I said them over and over to myself; and although that day was a great many years ago, I can still remember the lift I got as those words picked me up and stood me on my feet and sent me back to my task. Try saying over and over to yourself, "My God shall supply all [my] need," and see what it does for you.

The best way to read your Bible is to keep on in your reading until you come to something that seems to have been written just for you. It may be a word of guidance in your perplexity, or a word of faith for your fears, or a word of strength for your weakness. You have a feeling that God is speaking directly to you in those words. Stop right there and say them over and over to yourself. Keep on saying them until you know them by heart. "Be still, and know that I am God." "The Lord is the strength of my life." "If God be for us, who can be against us?" "When thou passest through the waters, I will be with thee; and through the rivers, they shall not overflow thee." Make a list of the verses that say to you the things you need to have said, and memorize them; and then when you come to the time for your prayer, visualize yourself in the presence of Christ and listen to them as they are spoken by him, and they will become a Word of God to your spirit. As more and more you read the Bible in this way, you will be surprised at the enthusiasm that comes from discovering new verses. You can build more and more alphabets of affirmations, according to the pattern in the last chapter

John Sutherland Bonnell tells about a young business woman in New York who took a taxi one morning for the office where she worked. After having driven a bit, the cab driver leaned back and remarked to her through the corner of his mouth, "New York is a ———— of a place to live in. Everybody is at everybody else's throat. People's nerves are on edge. It's confusion worse confounded. A man is crazy if he stays in this city if he has a chance of getting away from it."

The young woman smiled and said: "I don't blame you for feeling that way. I used to feel exactly that way myself."

"Don't you feel that way now?" asked the driver. Then, looking back at his passenger, he mumbled, "You don't quite look like a person that would have religion. Why don't you feel that way now?"

She said, "I don't know whether you would call it religon or not, but I have deep peace down inside me that I didn't use to have."

"How did you get it?" he asked.

"Every day I read my Bible," she said, "and I keep on reading it until I come to a verse that I feel is God's marching orders for the day. Usually I write this down

107

on a slip of paper and carry it with me. It keeps me steady whatever happens. It serves as a staff to lean on."

"Did you get a verse today?" asked the driver with heightened interest.

"Yes, I did," she replied, "and I have it right here. Only it begins to look as though this verse was intended for you instead of me. You have been talking about New York being a place where confusion is worse confounded. Well, listen to what it says." Opening her handbag, she took a slip of paper and read these words: "For God is not the author of confusion, but of peace" (I Cor. 14:33).

"Let me see that thing," said the driver, reaching back. She passed him the slip of paper; and as he drove along the street, he read it intently. Then he passed it back without a word of comment. They drove the rest of the trip in silence. As she was leaving the taxi, the young woman paid the driver and handed him a tip. Looking at her with a quiet smile on his face, he said: "Lady, I couldn't take a tip from you. You have given me something this morning worth more than all the tips I can earn today."

The president of a company sent his office boy out one day to bring him a Bible. The lad completed his errand and stood before his boss. "Young man," the boss said, "now you carry that book with ease; but when you get as old as I am, it will have to carry you." The Bible has always possessed carrying power; and when you find it for yourself, you will gain a new enthusiasm in your reading.

The same thing will happen to your experience of

prayer. When you begin to "wait on the Lord" in the sense of letting go, first, and then of letting God, you will receive such a lift that you literally cannot wait for the time to come when you can go "into the Presence" again. You will look forward to it just as now you look forward to your next meal. Muriel Lester, remember, put it like this: "I found my tiredness transformed into a deep restfulness." When you come to find in prayer a means of transforming your tiredness into restfulness and nerve tension into nerve tingling, you will feel different about it.

I used to wonder how our Lord could spend so much of his time praying. I read what Martin Luther said, that he had so much work to do some days that he couldn't get through the day without several hours of prayer. That was all so much Greek to me. I took great comfort in our Lord's words to the effect that we are not heard for our "much speaking." That seemed to give me authority for making short work of my prayers. But now I think I know why he would get up early and go up the mountain to pray, and why he would spend whole nights in prayer. His disciples said that, after he had been away in the secret place, there was a different look on his face. His countenance was changed. I have seen that happen too in the conference room, as in my visitor's face a look of tired tenseness gave way to a look of peace backed by power. Your countenance will change too when you find in prayer the power of God that floods your being with an exhilarating sense of new life.

Then there is another bit of lagniappe. In addition to

inner peace and a new enthusiasm for the practice of the presence of God in prayer and Bible reading, there is something else. Let us call it a practical method by means of which you can make the truth of your religion workable in experience.

Perhaps our biggest argument with religion is that we do not find it real. You hear the preacher say that if you will accept Christ you will find the answer for your needs. You can conquer fear, overcome a sense of inferiority, achieve peace of mind. But as far as you know, you have accepted Christ and still you lack the promise of your faith. What is wrong, and where can you find the solution?

The difficulty lies in the fact that, whereas your faith is intellectually valid, it has not become emotionally vivid. You do not consider a truth real until somehow you can feel its reality. You know that a thing is so; but unless you can feel it, it has no power for you.

For example, I sat down one day with a friend to talk about the unpardonable sin. The fear that he was guilty had made him sick, so sick that he had been to see a doctor and was threatened with having to give up his work. I thought I had the answer for him. I pointed out that the unpardonable sin is a nature so steeped in evil that it is incapable of knowing itself sinful, and therefore the fact that he felt guilty was proof that he was not. He said, "That seems to make sense, and I will go home and see what it will do for me."

But it did not do anything for him. He grew worse, and sometime later he came back. In the meantime I had had the experience described herein, and I began to

110

see why I had failed him. I had merely given him certain Christian truth for his mind and had not helped him make it real to his heart. What the Bible calls the "heart" is that part of the mind below the level of consciousness, and it is the "heart" that controls your disposition, your attitudes, the way you feel about things. Until the truth that you believe with the upper part of your mind, your understanding, is accepted by the under part of your mind, your subconscious self, it will never be real in the sense that it controls the way you feel. That is the reason why a certain man could say: "I do not believe in ghosts, but I am afraid of them just the same."

How then can you learn to believe with your deep mind? Our students of human nature tell us the answer is to say over and over to ourselves the things we wish to make real, just before we go to sleep at night and just after we wake up in the morning. The reason for that practice is that we are most relaxed from our tensions at those times, and the deep mind is most accessible when we are most relaxed. Taking a cue from that fact, I saw that if relaxation could be induced by certain exercises, then right there in my study my visitor's mind could be prepared for the planting of the seed of Christian truth, and it could be expected to bear fruit.

So when he came back a second time, instead of offering a reasonable explanation as to why he was not guilty of the unpardonable sin, I suggested that we pray. We then began to let go according to the plan already described. When his body and his mind had been relaxed, we visualized him as being in the presence of Christ. I had selected certain verses from the Bible that said the thing he needed to have made real to him, and we listened to these words as spoken by Christ. "Him that cometh to me I will in no wise cast out." "God so loved the world, that he gave his only begotten Son, that *whosoever* believeth in him should not perish, but have everlasting life." "He is able also to save them to the uttermost that come unto God by him." "Behold, I stand at the door, and knock: if *any* man hear my voice, and open the door, I will come in to him." I wrote these verses down on a piece of paper and suggested that he repeat the exercise two or three times a day. In that way truth that is intellectually valid can become emotionally vivid.

Whether the prayer was responsible for what happened, I do not know; but I do know that, whereas my friend was a spiritually sick person, now he is well again and happy in his Christian experience.

So it is that your faith can be made to work for you in any place of need. If your trouble is a nagging anxiety, use verses like this one: "I will fear no evil: for thou art with me." If your trouble is a haunting sense of inadequacy, use verses that affirm this fact: "I can do all things through Christ which strengtheneth me." Tell yourself that responsibility is simply your response to God's ability and that, if you will only do your best, he will do the rest. If your trouble is an inner restlessness that robs you of serenity, remember the word of the prophet: "Thou wilt keep him in perfect peace, whose mind is stayed on thee."

It will be a red-letter day in your life when you wake

intellectual and the moral and the spiritual will equip his people for their task of becoming better witnesses.

Herein lies the answer to a question that troubles the minds of many people today: Is it not selfish and therefore immoral to expect to get any help whatsoever from our religion? There are two mistakes we can make at this point. One is to seek to use God for our own happiness without accepting the obligations that his will imposes upon us; the other is to surrender dutifully but depressingly to the imperatives of that will without finding the "help of his countenance." The first is pure paganism, and it surely is not the religion of the Bible. God is not the servant of man, and faith is more than a selfish seeking for a solution to one's own ills. As the Westminster Shorter Catechism puts it, "Man's chief end is to glorify God, and to enjoy him forever"; and the popular parody of faith that teaches that "God's chief end is to glorify man and support him forever" deserves the judgment that it is receiving. But the second mistake is no less false than the first. God is neither the bellboy of our whims nor the "wholly other" of the Barthians. He is our Father; and while it is wrong certainly to make of faith a means of using God, it is also wrong to overlook the fact that the God of the Bible has promised provisions for our needs. Throughout the whole of the Old Testament prophet and psalmist alike sing a song that says, "The Lord is the strength of my life"; and in the New Testament we are told that we shall be "strengthened with might by [God's] Spirit in the inner man." We have no right to exploit the benefits of God for our own selfish purposes;

115

but once we have made ourselves the servants of the will of God, then we may rightfully accept his support.

I

In order to get this matter straight, notice, then, that throughout the Bible the promise of power is always tied to a commission. You remember the day when God called Moses in and said to him, "Come now therefore, and I will send thee unto Pharaoh, that thou mayest bring forth my people the children of Israel out of Egypt." Moses knew that Pharaoh was the mighty ruler of a world empire and that he himself was a nobody. He looked at that big job that had been placed upon his shoulders, and then he looked at his own little life, and he said: "Who am I [poor little me], that I should go unto Pharaoh, and that I should bring forth the children of Israel out of Egypt?" Then God spoke to him again, as much as to say: "Moses, you've got me wrong. I am not asking you to do this thing by yourself. I am telling you that, whenever I give a man a job to do, I always give him power to do it. Certainly, I will go with you." Moses received the promise of help, but it was tied to a commission.

In like manner, before our Lord set out upon his public ministry, he was baptized in the Jordan. At his baptism he heard a voice and he saw a vision. The voice confirmed his conviction that he was under commission as the messiah of God: "This is my beloved Son, in whom I am well pleased"; while the vision conveyed the promise of power: he saw the Spirit descending as a dove. Divine power for a divine task. The same fact is true when you think of the word of Jesus to his disciples. Before he was taken up out of their sight, he said to them: "You shall receive power when the Holy Spirit has come upon you, and you shall be my witnesses" (R.S.V.). The word "power" and the word "witnesses" go together. Power is always tied to a commission, and commitment always precedes the reception of power.

So it has ever been, and it will ever be thus. It is always a difficult thing in writing or speaking to use the personal pronoun of the first person, but one author uses the expression, "the stewardship of revealed truth." When God makes some of his truth known to a man, there comes a time when the man is under obligation to share it. In that spirit I want to let you know why I think it true that power is tied to a commission.

In 1922 at the age of sixteen I had what is known as a call to the ministry. There was no audible voice whatsoever; there was simply an inner conviction, which became more and more imperative, that my job was in the ministry. There was nothing in the world that I desired less. No member of my family had ever been in the ministry, and I looked upon it as the denial of all that a man might wish for. Moreover, I felt completely inadequate. I had always been plagued with a terrific timidity, and the idea of standing before an audience literally filled me with nausea. I knew exactly what the newspaper cartoon character Hambone meant when he said: "When I stands up to speak, my mind sits down on me." So lacking any desire to go into the ministry and plagued with a feeling of complete inadequacy, I tried my best to beg off. I said: "Lord, not the

117

ministry, above all things. If you will not insist, I will make a bargain with you: I will be a Sunday-school superintendent." But he was not interested in bargains. It was the ministry or nothing. And so in order to find any peace at all, I was forced to give in. I did so in the same mood with which Paul accepted his call: "Woe is unto me, if I preach not the gospel!"

That was in 1922. Three years later in the summer of 1925, between my junior and senior years in college, I accepted work in five little churches in Bossier Parish in Louisiana. I shall never forget the Saturday night before the first Sunday. Imagine how I felt! Here was a lad still in his teens, born with a timidity that was painful, knowing that next morning he would have to stand in a pulpit and deliver a sermon to the assembled congregation. If I had known anything about nervous breakdowns in those days, I am sure I would have had one.

I shall always remember the conversation we had that night, the Lord and I. I didn't pull any punches. I said, "Lord, this is your business, not mine. I didn't ask for this thing. I think you've shown mighty poor judgment in putting your finger on me. I tried to beg off, and you wouldn't let me. This is your little red wagon, and you've got to pull it. The responsibility is altogether yours; and if the sermon tomorrow morning is a flop, it's your fault."

I'll never forget as long as I live what he said in reply. It seemed to me he was saying something like this: "I'm glad you put it that way, about this job being my responsibility; for I want you to know that responsibility is nothing in the world but your response to my ability.

118

I'm willing to take the rap for what goes on tomorrow. I'm used to that sort of thing, because I spend my time taking the little that people can offer and backing it up. I'll make you this proposition: you do your best, and I'll do the rest." And I want to tell you that the next day, and every day since, I had the feeling that he was standing right there so close I could reach out and touch him, backing up his promise. Oftentimes the best I could offer was a poor second best, but from that day on he and I went to work on the basis of his proposition, and he has never yet let me down.

Herbert H. Farmer was right again. When God comes to meet a man, he comes in two ways, as "unconditional demand" and as "final succor." The demand was absolute: I could not shake it off; and the succor was sufficient: it has never ceased to see me through. All of which is another way of saying that the promise of power is always tied to a commission.

II

And I am quite sure it is within the meaning of the Bible to turn this truth around and put it like this: Not only is power tied to a commission, but a commission is tied to power. Commitment to the divine will is a condition for receiving divine power. But it is also true that, when in the course of events there is laid upon your life the necessity to do or to endure, the strength needed will be forthcoming.

For example, one of the giants who strides across the pages of the book of Acts with seven-league boots is a man named Paul. He had something that he called a "thorn in the flesh." He never did tell us what it was, which fact in itself is rather remarkable in the light of human nature's tendency to talk about its woes. He did say that he tried to get rid of it. Three times he prayed that God would take it away. He did not stop at three times, I am sure. After that he lost count. Finally, when he learned that he could not shake it off, God said to him, "My grace is sufficient for thee." Paul then settled down to make the most of it and to let it make the most for him. And he ended by saying this: "Most gladly therefore will I rather glory in my infirmities, that the power of Christ may rest upon me. . . . For when I am weak, then am I strong." Paul discovered that, when some duty was laid upon him to do or to endure, God stood by to give him power to see it through. He therefore handled his handicap handsomely, because he saw it in relation to his responsibility as a witness. "When I am weak," by virtue of my thorn in the flesh, "then am I strong," because of my opportunity to bear witness to what the power of God has done in my life. More power to you is for more power through you.

One day during World War II I met on the street a man who had two sons both of whom were with the army in Europe. His heart was heavy because his wife was ill and had no hope of recovery. His sons knew the burden he was carrying, and one of them had written to boost his morale. The letter had just arrived, and he stopped to read it to me. There was one sentence in it I'll never forget. What the boy said is worth remembering: "Dad, one thing I have learned over here is that

God never overloads anybody. He always gives you power to pull whatever he puts on you." In the midst of battle, bread; in the presence of struggle, strength! That is what the psalmist meant when he said: "Thou preparest a table before me in the presence of mine enemies." Not only is power tied to a commission, but a commission is tied to power.

Back in 1932 it was my pleasure to visit the lovely town of Moorefield in West Virginia, where I was the guest of the church for a week. One day we were riding down one of the streets when my friend the minister, John Chester Frist, pointed out a certain house. "Look at it," he said, "because I want to tell you a story about it." The story was this. During the days of the Civil War, Moorefield felt the force of the fighting. Being close to the border, one day it was in the hands of the Federal troops, the next it belonged to the Confederates. In that house an old lady lived alone. One morning early she heard a knock on the door. When she answered the knock, she found several soldiers of the enemy, who demanded breakfast. She told them to come in and she would have something on the table before too long. When the food was ready, she said to them: "It is a custom of long standing in this house to say prayers before breakfast. I hope you will not object." When they consented, she took her Bible and according to the signed testimony of the contemporary Presbyterian minister, opened it at random. She happened to turn to the twenty-seventh psalm and began reading.

The Lord is my light and my salvation; whom shall I fear? the Lord is the strength of my life; of whom shall I be afraid? When the wicked, even mine enemies and my foes, came upon me to eat up my flesh, they stumbled and fell. Though an host should encamp against me, my heart shall not fear: though war should rise against me, in this will I be confident. . . . And now shall mine head be lifted up above mine enemies round about me.

She read on through the last verse: "Wait on the Lord: be of good courage, and he shall strengthen thine heart." When she had finished the reading, she said, "Let us pray." While she was praying, she said she heard stealthy sounds as of men moving quietly about; and by the time she had said "Amen" and looked up, all the men had disappeared.

The story is a timeless parable: Bring God on the scene and the enemies of your well-being will fold their tents and silently steal away. Bring him on often enough and you will know that no task is too great and no testing too severe. You will never guess what God can do for you and through you until you tackle a task larger than you are, because when God gives a man a job to do, he always gives him power to do it.

One summer my family was at the beach on vacation, and I had taken along some books to read. One of these was called *The Servant of the Word* by the aforementioned Herbert H. Farmer. One day I was reading this book on the front porch of our cottage when a sentence suddenly stood out from the page. I went back and read it again, and what it said was this: "The true blessedness of life is in doing God's will and in the fellowship with him such doing brings." I knew that the word "blessed" means happy and that happiness is something most people are looking for; and I told myself that, if anybody is able to sum up its secret in a single sentence, it is worth remembering. Several times since that day I have gone back to read that sentence again and check on it, and I believe that it points straight to the one place where real happiness can be found: "The true blessedness of life is in doing God's will and in the fellowship with him such doing brings."

Many of us have consciences that make of the will of God an imperious commander, but not all of us know the blessedness that is waiting there for us. We are cheating ourselves when we see the duty and miss the beauty, for in that fellowship there is power and there is peace. Once you know it, you cannot keep it to yourself, and you will become a witness.

III

There is another meaning wrapped up in this word "witnesses": Once we have felt within ourselves and know firsthand the power of God, then our witnessing will carry conviction and get results.

There is one thing in Luke's story of the Acts that he does not tell us and that I would like to know: Was the maid who was present in the high priest's court present that day on the street in Jerusalem when Peter and John stood up to the authorities? The last time she saw Peter, he was as weak as water and denied his Lord; this time he is a new man. This time he is standing up before the most powerful authorities in the city, who demand that he say not another word about his Lord, and answering like this: "You can try to shut us up if you like, but there is one thing I want you to know: We must obey God rather than men like yourselves." What had happened was that in between those two events Peter had come into possession of the power of God. He now had inside information and knew what he was talking about; and if the maid was there, I am sure she was impressed by that witnessing.

E. Stanley Jones reports that in one of his conferences a minister said this: "When I preach something ahead of what I am, I only irritate people; but when I preach what I have experienced, I inspire people."

It is ever thus. Let some man, beaten down by his business or his marriage or his foolish habits, come to his minister for help. If the minister has never known within himself anything of the power of God and says to his visitor, "Man, what you need to do is to pray about this thing," the man will know that he has come to the wrong place for help. But if that man of God knows anything of the power of God; if prayer for him has been a plugging in on divine resources, if his life is a channel into which a strength stronger than his own has been flowing, then it will flow on through and touch the other. And when he says to his visitor, "My friend, let us take a few minutes and kneel down and close our eyes and open the door into the unseen and let Christ come in and put his hand upon our shoulders and his strength into our need," when that man gets up to leave, he will know that he has been in touch with the power of God, and as he walks he goes not alone; there are two, and the other is God.

One of the most amazing operations of the power

of God in contemporary life is in an organization of men and women known as Alcoholics Anonymous. Their program is based upon twelve steps, the second of which says this: "We came to believe that a Power greater than ourselves could restore us to sanity."

The monthly magazine of the organization is called *The Grapevine,* and in the issue of December, 1955, there is a picture that shows two members making a call upon a friend. The object of their visit gives every evidence that his life has become unmanageable. He is half-clothed, sitting on the edge of the bed; his hair is rumpled; and the bottle on the table is uncorked and empty. The neat appearance of his visitors contrasts with his own dishevelment, and on their faces is the look of calm confidence that comes from being in touch with power. On his own countenance there is a glimmer of hope, and underneath the picture are the words "Came to believe . . ." He came to believe in a power that could restore him to sanity when he met two men who possessed that power.

"You shall receive power when the Holy Spirit has come upon you, and you shall be my witnesses." There can be no doubt about it: The Witness of the Church will become effective when the world finds in its ministers and its members men and women who themselves know something of the power of God.

Let God help you; yes, but that is only the beginning. More power to you is always for more power *through* you.